KIDS'FIELD GUIDES

Birds

of North America EAST

Jo S. Kittinger

SMITHSONIAN

LONDON, NEW YORK, SYDNEY, DELHI, PARIS,
MUNICH, and JOHANNESBURG

Editor-in-Chief Russell Greenberg, Ph.D.
Director of the Migratory Bird Center at the National Zoological Park

Publisher Andrew Berkhut
Project Editor Andrea Curley
Art Director Tina Vaughan
Jacket Designer Karen Shooter

Produced by Southern Lights Custom Publishing
Editorial Director Shelley DeLuca
Production Director Lee Howard
Art Director Miles Parsons
President Ellen Sullivan

Editorial Consultants
Joseph DiCostanzo
Alice S. Christenson, Frank Farrell III, Shirley J. Farrell
Dana Hamilton, Stan Hamilton, Greg Harber

First American Edition, 2001
00 01 02 03 04 05 10 9 8 7 6 5 4 3 2 1
Published in the United States by
DK Publishing, Inc.
95 Madison Avenue, New York, New York 10016
Copyright © 2001 DK Publishing, Inc. and Smithsonian Institution

The name of the Smithsonian Institution and the sunburst logo
are registered trademarks of the Smithsonian Institution.

Library of Congress Cataloging-in-Publication Data
Kittinger, Jo S.
Birds of North America. East / by Jo S. Kittinger.--1st American ed.
p. cm. -- (Smithsonian kid's field guides)
ISBN 0-7894-7899-4 (pp) ISBN 0-7894-7898-6 (lib. bdg.)
1. Birds--East (U.S.)--Identification--Juvenile literature. 2. Birds--Canada,
Eastern--Identification--Juvenile literature. [1. Birds--Identification.] I. Title. II. Series.

QL683.E27 K58 2001
598'.0974--dc21   2001028429

Printed and bound in Italy by Graphicom, srl.
Color reproduction by Colourscan, Singapore.

see our complete catalog at
www.dk.com

Contents

How to Use this Book 4

About Birds 6

Identifying Birds 8

Watching Birds 12

Bringing Birds Home 14

Bird Descriptions 16

Long-legged Waders 16–23

Ducks and Other Swimming Birds 24–40

Birds of Shore and Sea 41–59

Chickenlike Birds 60–63

Pigeons and Doves 64–65

Birds of Prey 66–79

Nightjars 80–81

Swifts and Hummingbirds 82–83

Woodpeckers 84–89

Flycatchers and Other Picky Eaters 90–98

Jays and Crows 99–100

Songbirds 101–131

Sparrows and Finches 132–147

Blackbirds 148–155

Glossary 156

Index 159

How to Use This Book

Using this book, you will learn to identify 140 birds that you might find near you in eastern North America. Each page tells what the bird looks like, where it lives, how it sounds, and what it eats.

THE PICTURES

The photos in this book show you the colors of a bird's feathers in spring and summer, called breeding plumage. This is when birds reproduce, or breed. When males and females look very different at this time, you will see a photo of each. When birds are finished breeding, they grow their winter plumage. Like the goldfinch at right, some can look different in winter. Also, a young bird, called a juvenile, can look different from its parents. Some birds, such as gulls, take up to four years to look like an adult. Drawings like these show these differences.

Winter male

Winter female

Juvenile

THE MAP

Each page has a map like this. The colors tell you what time of year that bird might be in your area. But remember that although some birds stay in one place all year, others move around. This is called migration. If you live somewhere in between two colors, you might see that bird during migration in the spring and fall.

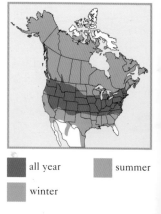

all year   summer

winter

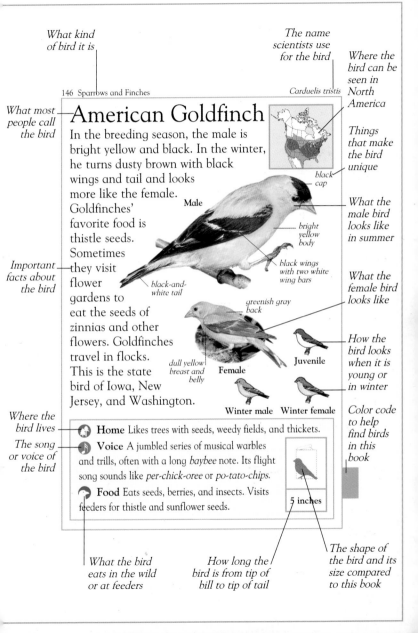

What kind of bird it is

The name scientists use for the bird

Where the bird can be seen in North America

Carduelis tristis

What most people call the bird

American Goldfinch

In the breeding season, the male is bright yellow and black. In the winter, he turns dusty brown with black wings and tail and looks more like the female. Goldfinches' favorite food is thistle seeds. Sometimes they visit flower gardens to eat the seeds of zinnias and other flowers. Goldfinches travel in flocks. This is the state bird of Iowa, New Jersey, and Washington.

Things that make the bird unique

black cap

Male

What the male bird looks like in summer

bright yellow body

black wings with two white wing bars

Important facts about the bird

black-and-white tail

greenish gray back

What the female bird looks like

dull yellow breast and belly

Female

Juvenile

How the bird looks when it is young or in winter

Winter male   Winter female

Color code to help find birds in this book

Where the bird lives

🔵 **Home** Likes trees with seeds, weedy fields, and thickets.

The song or voice of the bird

🔵 **Voice** A jumbled series of musical warbles and trills, often with a long *baybee* note. Its flight song sounds like *per-chick-oree* or *po-tato-chips.*

🔵 **Food** Eats seeds, berries, and insects. Visits feeders for thistle and sunflower seeds.

5 inches

What the bird eats in the wild or at feeders

How long the bird is from tip of bill to tip of tail

The shape of the bird and its size compared to this book

About Birds

There are more than 9,000 species of birds in the world. They all have several things in common. All birds are warm-blooded. All birds are covered with feathers. All birds have two legs, usually covered with scaly skin. All birds have two wings, but not all birds can fly. All birds have a bill, but no teeth. All birds lay eggs.

long, curved neck

tail bone

ankle joint

knee joint

breastbone holds the wing muscles

legs bend backward

BONES
A bird has bones strong enough to hold it up, yet light enough for it to fly. Most birds that fly have hollow bones.

Down

Contour

Flight
(Wing and tail)

FEATHERS
Feathers keep a bird warm and help it fly. There are three types of feathers: down, contour, and flight feathers. Fluffy down feathers, which grow next to the skin, keep the bird warm. Contour feathers cover most of the body. Flight feathers help the bird fly.

BILLS

Birds use their bills to clean themselves, to build a nest, and to eat. The shape of the bill determines what the bird can eat.

Osprey
Birds of prey use their strong, hooked bills to eat meat or fish.

American Robin
Thrushes and other songbirds use their pointed bills to pick up berries and insects.

Northern Shoveler

Ducks, which strain food out of the water, have flat bills.

LEGS AND FEET

Bird legs are thin but strong. Most birds have four toes, with three toes pointing forward and one turned to the back. A claw is on each toe. A bird's feet are made for its lifestyle, whether that is perching, hunting, or swimming.

The American Robin has three toes forward and one toe back for perching on branches.

The Osprey has claws, called talons, that are good for holding its prey.

The Northern Shoveler has webs between three toes to help the duck paddle through water.

Identifying Birds

Most birds do not sit still for long. To identify birds it is important to notice details quickly. Practice asking yourself these questions, because the answers are what you need to name the birds you see.

WHAT SHAPE AND SIZE IS THE BIRD?
The first things you should look at are a bird's shape and size. This will help you place the bird in a family group and locate it in this book, using the symbols in the bottom right corner of the page.

WHAT COLORS ARE THE FEATHERS?
Is the bird blue or brown? This can point you in the right direction, but it is also important to notice whether the feathers are spotted, streaked, or plain.

spotted   streaked   plain and unmarked

WHAT DOES THE HEAD LOOK LIKE?
Look at the shape and the markings.

The point on top of the Northern Cardinal's head is called a crest.

The Loggerhead Shrike looks like it is wearing a mask on its face.

WHAT DOES THE BILL LOOK LIKE?

Look at the shape and the color.

The American Coot is a gray ducklike bird with a white bill.

The Common Snipe's bill is twice as long as its head.

WHAT DO THE LEGS LOOK LIKE?

Look at the color.

The Great Egret holds its black legs behind its body when it flies.

The Herring Gull has pink legs.

WHAT DO THE WINGS LOOK LIKE?

Look at the shape, size, and markings.

A Chimney Swift has long, narrow wings.

The large white patches on the Northern Mockingbird's wings make the bird easy to identify in flight.

WHAT DOES THE TAIL LOOK LIKE?

Look at the shape, size, and markings.

The Pied-billed Grebe has a short gray tail with white feathers underneath it.

The American Redstart has large yellow patches on its fan-shaped tail.

HABITS

While you look at a bird, you should also notice what it is doing. Like people who do things such as tugging their hair or tapping their fingers, birds do things that can be great clues to their identity. Does the bird hover in the air? Does it wag its tail? Does it climb up, or down, a tree? All of these habits, or behaviors, can help you learn a bird's identity.

Hummingbirds hover while they feed.

Nuthatches climb head first down trees.

The Northern Parula's song sounds like zeeeeee-yip!

🎵 VOICE

Experienced birdwatchers can identify birds by their song or call. Not all birds sing, but most of them do make noise. Many birds have a call, which is different from the song. A call is simple and might mean the bird is frightened. Birds may use calls to communicate. In this book you can read about a bird's song where you see the symbol above.

FOOD

Birds live in places where they can find the food they need to survive. Some birds pick fruits and berries from trees. Others look in or near the water for food. Find out what a bird eats where you see the symbol above.

Sanderlings are often seen on saltwater beaches, looking for food at the edge of the water.

HOME

Most birds have a particular place where they like to live, called a habitat. The beach is a habitat of sand, saltwater, and the plants and animals that live there. Identifying birds is easier if you learn which birds to expect in different habitats. After you look at the range map on each page to see where a bird lives, read about its habitat where you see the symbol above. But remember that during migration birds can appear in unlikely places.

Flocks of American Crows gather in large, open places such as prairies or fields.

Watching Birds

Watching birds, "birding," is something you can do anywhere. The best times are early in the morning or late in the afternoon, when birds are most active. Remember to be as still and quiet as you can, because

A pair of binoculars will help you see birds up close.

quick moves and noise will scare birds away. It is also helpful if you wear dull colors so you will blend in with nature. Be sure to take along this book, binoculars, and a notebook and pencil.

PATTERNS IN THE AIR

Many birds fly straight ahead, flapping their wings the whole time. This is true of ducks, doves, crows, and many songbirds. The heavier a bird is, the faster it needs to fly to stay in the air.

Some birds flap their wings several times, then glide. This helps save energy. Birds that flap and glide are hawks, owls, vultures, and pelicans.

Many smaller birds, such as woodpeckers and chickadees, hold their wings close to their bodies as they pause and glide between flaps. This makes them fly up and down like a roller coaster.

KEEP YOUR DISTANCE
Watching birds is fun, but you do not want to get too close. If you find a bird's nest, be sure to watch it from a distance. Do not touch it. Birders are always careful not to disturb wildlife of any kind.

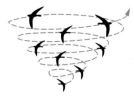

Another way some birds save energy is by soaring. Large hawks, eagles, vultures, and gulls ride upward on heated air (which rises) or drafts.

Certain types of birds can flap their wings rapidly while staying in the same place in the air. Hummingbirds do this

while gathering flower nectar. Some birds of prey, such as the American Kestrel, hover in the air while looking for food.

Some birds fly in straight lines or V-shaped patterns to help save energy. By riding on the air flowing from the bird in front of it, the bird behind does not have to flap its wings as hard.

Bringing Birds Home

Attracting birds to your backyard will let you enjoy their habits, colors, and songs. By putting out food, water, and shelter you can help provide a good habitat for these beautiful creatures.

FOOD

Invite birds to your yard with food. The foods you can put out to attract them are listed in the bird descriptions. Some birds like to eat on the ground. Others will come to feeders that are filled with seeds, suet, or nectar. Many types of birdfeeders are available at stores.

American Goldfinches eat at feeders that are filled with thistle or sunflower seeds.

Woodpeckers such as this Downy Woodpecker will come to eat from your suet feeder.

Many birds, such as these Mourning Doves, prefer to eat their food on the ground. No feeder is required – just throw down some black oil sunflower seeds and watch the birds eat.

WATER

Do not forget water! Birds need a supply of water for drinking and bathing. Regular baths help a bird keep itself clean and maintain its feathers.

SHELTER

Before you can give birds a home, you need to find out what kinds of birds in your area might use it. Different families of birds make different sizes and shapes of nests. They use all kinds of nest-building materials. You can help birds build a cozy nest by putting nesting materials such as string or dryer lint outside where birds can find it. Look in books or on the Internet to find instructions for all types of nest boxes.

Bluebirds depend on nest boxes like this one for a place to raise their young. Inside the nest box, the baby birds wait for a meal.

Ardea herodias

Great Blue Heron

This bird is the largest heron in North America. Like all herons, it flies with its neck held in an S-shape. A heron usually stands very still in the water before stabbing prey with its daggerlike bill.

black crown

yellowish bill

dark streaks on whitish neck

bluish gray body

long yellow-green legs

Juvenile

In flight the heron's long legs reach far past its tail.

Home Lives near shallow water of rivers, lakes, swamps, and ponds. Also lives along the coast. Sometimes it may be seen walking in grassy fields near water. Many pairs of birds make their nests close together in the same tree.

Voice Usually silent except around other herons, when it makes squawks and low croaks.

Food Eats fish, frogs, salamanders, snakes, grasshoppers, mice, dragonflies, and squirrels.

46–52 inches

Great Egret

In January both the male and female
Great Egret grow long, white
plumes on their backs to
attract a mate. The birds
shed their beautiful
plumes by summer
and do not have
any for the rest
of the year.

yellow bill

*black legs
and feet*

*long, slender
neck*

At one time, so
many egrets were
killed for these
plumes, which
were used to
decorate women's
hats, that this bird
almost became extinct.

*slender white
body*

Home Lives near freshwater ponds and
marshes. Also lives near saltwater marshes as well
as along the coast.

Voice Croaks loudly or says *cuk, cuk.*

Food Eats fish, frogs, snakes, crayfish, and
large insects.

**37–41
inches**

Bubulcus ibis

Cattle Egret

You might see this bird riding on the back of a cow. As the cattle walk and graze, they flush insects out of the grass. This is one way the Cattle Egret gets its food – and how it got its name. This small member of the heron family moved here to North America from other parts of the world all by itself, which is unusual. Many other "introduced" birds living here in the wild were brought here by people.

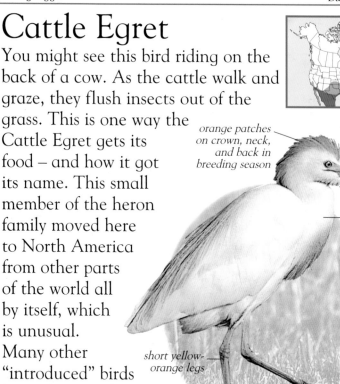

orange patches on crown, neck, and back in breeding season

yellow-orange bill

short, thick neck

short yellow-orange legs

Juvenile

🏠 **Home** Lives near fields and pastures. Also lives in mangroves near the coast.

🎵 **Voice** Usually silent, but makes croaking sounds near the nest.

🍴 **Food** Eats grasshoppers and other insects in grassy fields. Also eats insects and grubs found on ground that has just been plowed.

19–21 inches

Green Heron

This bird is a natural fisherman. The Green Heron will actually place some bait – a feather or twig – in the water to lure fish and other small prey, such as frogs. The Green Heron eats alone or in pairs. It can stand still for minutes at a time while looking for food. The bird might raise the crest of dark green feathers on its head when it is nervous or excited.

dark green head

crest that can be raised

blue-green back

thin brownish yellow bill

chestnut neck

yellow or orange legs

Juvenile

🌲 **Home** Lives near wetlands, including swamps, marshes, ponds, and wooded streams.

🎵 **Voice** Sounds like *kyowk* or *skeow* or a quieter *kuck, kuck*.

🌙 **Food** Eats mostly small fish but also eats insects and frogs.

18–22 inches

Black-crowned Night-Heron

This active night hunter sometimes flies to the nests of other birds to eat their young. You might see a large colony roosting together in trees during the day. Conservation groups are trying to protect the night-heron, but its wetland habitats are shrinking. A similar bird, the Yellow-crowned Night-Heron, lives in the Southeast. It has a yellowish stripe on its crown, a black face, and a gray back.

black cap

red eyes

heavy, sharply pointed bill

white face, chest, and belly

black back

yellow legs and feet

Juvenile

🏠 **Home** Lives in wetlands, marshes, swamps, streams near woods, and near the coast.

🎵 **Voice** Sounds like a loud *quock* or *quaik*.

🌓 **Food** Prefers small fish but also eats snakes, frogs, mice, and sometimes young birds. This bird also walks through tall grass, looking for mice.

25–28 inches

White Ibis

Ancient cultures, including the
Egyptians, honored the ibis.
Sometimes birds belonging to the ibis
family were mummified and buried in temples with
Egyptian leaders. Ibises fly in loose lines that can
stretch more than a mile long. In flight the White
Ibis's black wing tips show. This bird uses its long,
curved bill to probe in the
mud for food while
walking slowly in
shallow water.

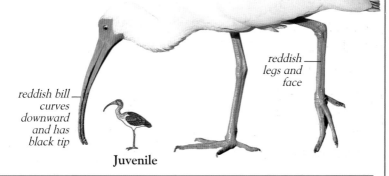

all-white body

reddish legs and face

reddish bill curves downward and has black tip

Juvenile

🌲 **Home** Lives near marshes inland and near
the coast. Nests, roosts, and feeds in large flocks.

🎵 **Voice** Males call *hunk-hunk-hunk-hunk*.
Females make a squealing sound.

🪱 **Food** Eats crayfish, crabs, small fish, frogs,
small snakes, and insects.

21–27 inches

Wood Stork

This is the only stork that is native to North America. It flies with its neck straight out and long legs straight behind. It is endangered because the shallow wetland habitat where it lives is being destroyed. The Wood Stork is nicknamed "flinthead," because its gray head and upper neck are the color of a type of gray stone called flint.

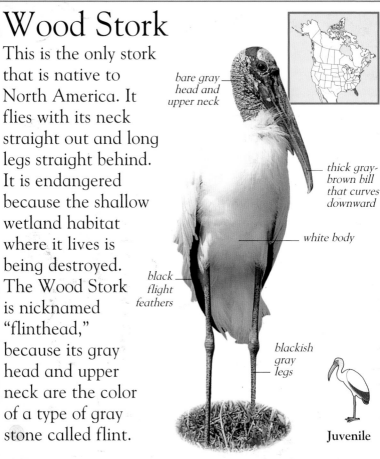

bare gray head and upper neck

thick gray-brown bill that curves downward

white body

black flight feathers

blackish gray legs

Juvenile

🌲 **Home** Lives on or near the southeastern coast. Often many birds are found nesting together in a colony.

🎵 **Voice** Mostly silent. Clatters and snaps bill.

🐾 **Food** Walks or wades in water up to its belly, probing underwater with its long bill for fish, frogs, young alligators, and bugs.

35–45 inches

Sandhill Crane

This is the only crane that can be found in many places across North America. It flies with its neck held straight out in front. In spring these birds pair off and do an amazing dance. They jump in the air, spread their wings, and call loudly. Another member of the crane family is the larger Whooping Crane, which is white with black wing tips and a black mustache. The Whooping Crane is endangered.

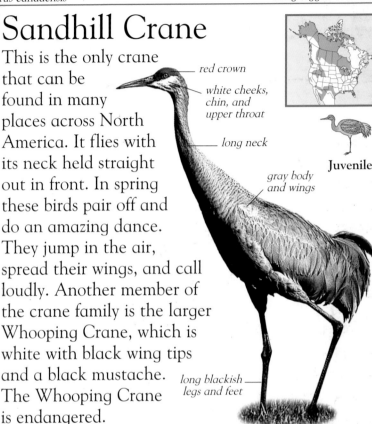

red crown

white cheeks, chin, and upper throat

long neck

Juvenile

gray body and wings

long blackish legs and feet

🏠 **Home** Lives near shallow ponds, marshes, lakes with forests nearby, and damp meadows.

🎵 **Voice** Its loud, trumpetlike *garoo-oo-a-a-a-a* can be heard from more than a mile away.

🦅 **Food** Eats small birds, snakes, lizards, frogs, mice, and crayfish. Also eats water plants, berries, seeds, and grains.

34–48 inches

Common Loon

A loon can see underwater. This is helpful, because a loon can dive as deep as 200 feet below the surface and can stay underwater for as long as three minutes. Since loons spend so much time on lakes, a healthy loon can be a sign of clean water. This is the state bird of Minnesota and the official bird of Ontario.

shiny black head with green gloss

checkered black-and-white back

striped white neck

white breast and belly

In winter another member of the loon family, the Red-throated Loon, looks like a small Common Loon with a plain gray back.

Winter adult

🏠 **Home** Lives in lakes and rivers near forests in summer. In winter, moves to the ocean or coast.

🎵 **Voice** Known for the spooky laughing sounds it makes. Also yodels, sounding like *ha-oo-oo*.

🐚 **Food** Eats fish, shrimp, snails, and frogs.

28–36 inches

Pied-billed Grebe

This common bird can hide by sinking slowly under the water until only its head is showing. It is the only grebe that does this, but all grebes can dive underwater so fast they are called "water witch" and "devil-diver." In winter its chin turns white, and the ring around its bill disappears.

large head

white tail "puff"

short neck

dark ring on short, thick bill

brownish body

Winter adult

🌲 **Home** Lives in ponds and marshes in spring, where it hides its floating nest in the water plants. Migrates to spend winter on large lakes or the ocean.

🎵 **Voice** Loud, cuckoolike call of *cuck, cuck, cuck, cow-cow-cow, cow-ah-cow-ah.*

🍂 **Food** Dives underwater with amazing speed to catch bugs and fish.

12–15 inches

Pelecanus occidental.

Brown Pelican

Even though you might see a lot of Brown Pelicans near the beach, this bird is endangered. Now that certain pesticides are being used less often, the Brown Pelican is increasing in number. This is one of two kinds of pelicans in North America. It is the only one that flies above the water and dives down to scoop up fish with the large pouch in its bill. The Brown Pelican is the state bird of Louisiana.

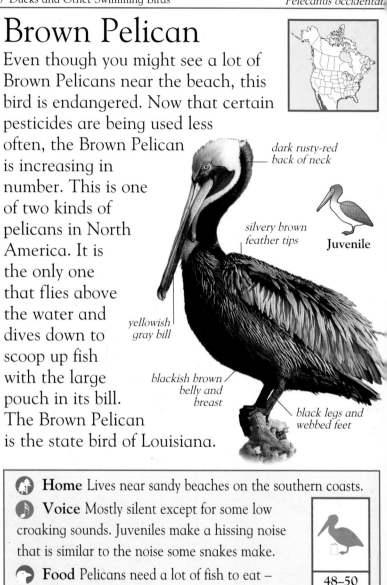

dark rusty-red back of neck

silvery brown feather tips

Juvenile

yellowish gray bill

blackish brown belly and breast

black legs and webbed feet

🏠 **Home** Lives near sandy beaches on the southern coasts.

🎵 **Voice** Mostly silent except for some low croaking sounds. Juveniles make a hissing noise that is similar to the noise some snakes make.

🐟 **Food** Pelicans need a lot of fish to eat – about four pounds a day.

48–50 inches

Double-crested Cormorant

A cormorant may look like a duck, but it is more closely related to a pelican. Like the pelican, a cormorant has webs on its feet that reach to its toes. Unlike pelicans and ducks, a cormorant's wings are not waterproof. After it is done fishing, a cormorant has to go ashore, where it perches with its wings open so they can dry. Then the bird can fly well again.

tufts in breeding season

bright yellow-orange throat pouch

brown back with black feathers

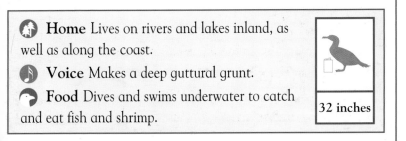

🌲 **Home** Lives on rivers and lakes inland, as well as along the coast.

🎵 **Voice** Makes a deep guttural grunt.

🐟 **Food** Dives and swims underwater to catch and eat fish and shrimp.

32 inches

Anhinga

An Anhinga usually swims with its whole body underwater up to its neck. Its long thin neck and small narrow head make the bird look like a snake in the water. The Anhinga's wings are not waterproof, so it must spread its wings to dry in the sun after swimming. This is also true of cormorants, which are more common than the Anhinga.

Female

pale head, neck, and breast

dark-brown body

black neck and head

silver streaks

black feathers with green shine

long fanlike tail

Male

🏠 **Home** Lives near the coast in the Southeast.

🎵 **Voice** Usually silent, but if face-to-face with another bird it makes a rapid clicking that sounds like *guk-guk-guk-guk-guk*.

🌓 **Food** Spears fish with its pointed bill while swimming underwater. Also eats insects and frogs.

35 inches

Snow Goose

This bird comes in two different color morphs. There is a completely white one with black tips on its wings and a dark one with a bluish gray upper body and brownish gray lower body. The dark morph is called the "Blue Goose." The Snow Goose often feeds in fields far away from water.

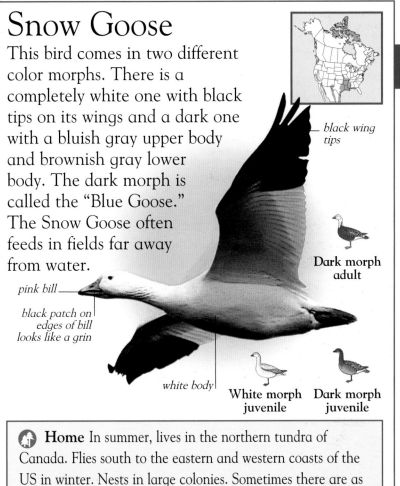

black wing tips

Dark morph adult

pink bill

black patch on edges of bill looks like a grin

white body

White morph juvenile

Dark morph juvenile

🚶 **Home** In summer, lives in the northern tundra of Canada. Flies south to the eastern and western coasts of the US in winter. Nests in large colonies. Sometimes there are as many as 1,200 nests in one square mile.

🎵 **Voice** Makes either shrill or soft honks. In flight it makes a barking sound.

🌀 **Food** Eats tender plants and grains in winter. Digs up and eats roots of water plants in summer.

25–31 inches

Canada Goose

If you hear honking and look up to
see several geese flying in a V shape,
they are probably Canada Geese.
They come in different sizes, and
some people call the bigger geese
"honkers." There are more of this
species than any other kind
of geese, and they are
probably increasing
in numbers.

white "strap" on chin

brownish gray back

paler brown sides

light-colored belly

🐾 **Home** Lives anywhere near the water. Can
be seen in parks, yards, and on golf courses while
they are migrating in the fall and spring.

🎵 **Voice** Deep, musical *honk-a-lonk*.

● **Food** Eats fresh grasses and other plants.

25–45 inches

Mute Swan

People brought this graceful bird from Europe to live in ponds and parks in New England. The Mute Swan is not really "mute," as its name suggests. It does make some noises. The swan defends its nest by hissing and chasing off visitors, especially dogs and people. In winter, a similar native bird called the Tundra Swan can be found in the same marshes.

Juvenile

long neck

orange bill with large black knob

all-white body

🏠 **Home** Lives on lakes and ponds in parks or yards. In the wild it lives near lakes, ponds, and rivers, mostly near the East Coast. Also found around the Great Lakes.

🎵 **Voice** Usually silent but sometimes makes hisses, barks, and snorts.

🌓 **Food** Sticks its long neck underwater to eat the plants that grow on the bottom.

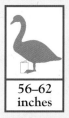

56–62 inches

Wood Duck

The colorful Wood Duck is named for the wooded habitat where it lives. It is called a "perching duck" because it perches in trees. Sharp claws help the Wood Duck hold onto branches. Like most other ducks, the female Wood Duck is less colorful than her mate.

gray head

white circle around the eyes

brownish chest

Female

Juvenile

big pointed crest

blue-green back

red, white, black, and yellow bill

Male

dark-red chest with white spots

long tail

yellowish sides

🏠 **Home** Lives near wooded rivers, ponds, and swamps. Visits marshes in summer and fall. Nests in tree cavities. Also uses nest boxes people make for them.

🎵 **Voice** Male whistles a soft *jeee?* or *ter-weeee?* Female loudly says *wooo-eek!*

🍴 **Food** Eats water plants, snails, tadpoles, salamanders, acorns, seeds, and grains.

17–20 inches

Mallard

This familiar duck can be found near shallow freshwater almost anywhere in North America. The shiny green head, purplish breast, and white collar of the male are in sharp contrast to the dull brown spotted feathers of the female.

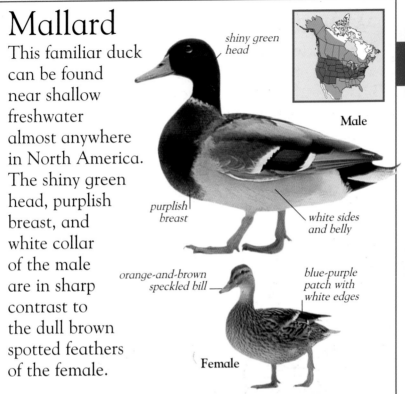

shiny green head

Male

purplish breast

white sides and belly

orange-and-brown speckled bill

blue-purple patch with white edges

Female

🌲 **Home** Lives near ponds, marshes, and lakes. Tame Mallards can be found on any body of water, sometimes even in city parks, pastures, or alfalfa fields.

🎵 **Voice** Female has a loud *quack-quack-quack* that sounds softer the longer she speaks. Male makes a double *kwek-kwek-kwek*.

🌑 **Food** Dabbles, or turns upside down, in shallow water to find plants and insects. Also looks for food on the shore or in a nearby field.

23 inches

Northern Shoveler

The shoveler has a bill that is longer and wider than any other duck's bill. It is shaped like a shovel with ridges on the side. The bird pushes it through the water to find food.

Male

black head with green shine

white tail feathers

white spot on flank

rusty red sides and belly

Three or four shovelers may swim in a circle so they can eat the food stirred up by the feet in front of them.

gray bill with orange speckles

brown speckled back

Female

🌲 **Home** Needs water to find food. Spends winter in freshwater marshes. Nests in spring in small ponds or prairie potholes.

🎵 **Voice** Usually quiet but sometimes makes low quacking sounds.

🦜 **Food** Eats water plants and animals.

17–20 inches

Lesser Scaup

This expert diver is common in North America. In winter, scaups float on the water in a large flock called a "raft." Like other diving ducks, a scaup needs a running start on the water before it can take off. A similar duck, the Greater Scaup, might be seen with Lesser Scaups in winter but it is less common.

white on face

brown body

Female

pointed black head

gray back

bluish gray bill has black tip

Male

black chest

🏠 **Home** Lives near ponds and marshes, as well as in bays and inlets. In the winter, visits lakes and rivers.

🎵 **Voice** The male whistles a low *whew* when looking for a mate. The female purrs *kwuh-h-h-h*.

🍽 **Food** Eats weeds, grass, snails, shrimplike crustaceans, and water insects.

15–18 inches

Bucephala albeola

Bufflehead

The Bufflehead is the smallest diving duck. It can take off directly from the water, which is unusual because most diving ducks need to get a running start on the water first. Buffleheads do not form large flocks in winter like some diving ducks. When looking for a mate, the male puts on a show, bobbing his head up and down.

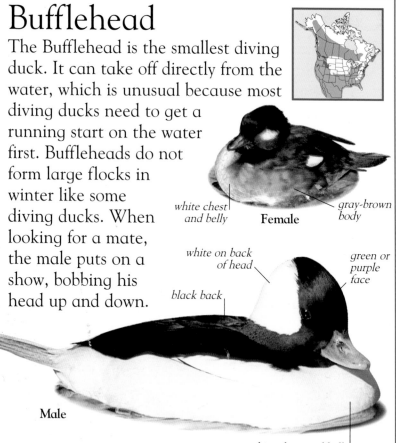

white chest and belly

Female

gray-brown body

white on back of head

green or purple face

black back

Male

white chest and belly

🏕️ **Home** Likes to spend winters on the coast. In summer, lives near ponds, lakes, and rivers.

🎵 **Voice** Has a squeaky whistle and sometimes makes a low squealing or growling. Females quack.

🌊 **Food** Dives for water insects, snails, small fish, underwater plant seeds, and shrimp.

13–16 inches

Common Merganser

Of all the ducks that dive into the water to catch and eat fish, the merganser is the largest. Its narrow bill has "teeth" on the sides that help this bird hold onto slippery fish. Because of these teeth some people call the Common Merganser by the nickname "Sawbill."

tufted chestnut head

gray body

white chin

Female

glossy green head

black back

thin red bill

Male

long body

white belly and chest

🌲 **Home** Lives near freshwater lakes, ponds, and rivers surrounded by trees. Makes its nest in a tree or on the ground near water. Some use an old hawk or flicker nest.

🎵 **Voice** Male croaks harshly. Female loudly says *karr karr*.

🐟 **Food** Eats mostly fish, especially minnows, plus eels, frogs, salamanders, and water insects.

22–27 inches

Oxyura jamaicensis

Ruddy Duck

This little diving duck can sink slowly underwater and disappear without leaving any ripples in the water. It uses its long, stiff tail to steer in the water like a boat uses a rudder. The Ruddy Duck is better suited for swimming than walking. Its legs are so far back on its body that it is almost helpless on land.

brown-gray back

blackish gray bill

Female

white cheeks

blackish head

Male

blue bill

long, stiff tail

rust-colored body

whitish belly

Winter male

🌲 **Home** Lives near marshes surrounded by cattails and reeds. Also along the coast during winter.

🎵 **Voice** Mostly silent, but a male trying to find a mate says *chuck-chuck-chuck-chuck-churr.*

🐦 **Food** Dives into water to find shellfish and water plants. Also eats grass found in ponds.

14–16 inches

Purple Gallinule

Because it has huge feet, the Purple Gallinule is able to walk on top of the lily pads in its marshy home. When it swims, this colorful bird pumps its head back and forth.

pale-blue patch above bill

bright-purple head

brownish green back

white feathers under tail

red bill with yellow tip

purple chest and belly

Spotting a Purple Gallinule can be hard because it is shy and much of its habitat is disappearing.

very long yellow legs

large yellow feet

Juvenile

🌲 **Home** Lives in swamps and marshes.

🎵 **Voice** Shrieks, chatters, and clucks. Sometimes says *kr'lik'* or *kee-k'*.

🐦 **Food** Visits rice fields to feed on seeds and grains. This bird also eats water plants, water insects, and snails.

13–14 inches

American Coot

Even though it looks like a duck, this is a member of the rail family. Coots are usually seen in large flocks swimming on large bodies of water. The American Coot pumps its head back and forth while it is swimming.

reddish brown patch on forehead

gray-black head and neck

short white bill

dark-gray body

This bird is a bit of a bully and sometimes steals from other birds that dive into the water for food.

Juvenile

🏠 **Home** Lives near marshes, lakes, ponds, rivers, and coasts.

🎵 **Voice** Cackles, whistles, and grunts while splashing in water. Also says *coo-coo-coo-coo*.

🌐 **Food** Dives 10–25 feet below water for plants, small fish, tadpoles, snails, and worms.

15 inches

Semipalmated Plover

You are most likely to see this small shorebird when it migrates. In spring and fall, flocks move between their summer breeding grounds in the Far North and their winter home on southern beaches.

faint eye ring

brown back

orange bill with black tip

broad black collar

white chest and belly

A Semipalmated Plover searches for its food by running, then stopping suddenly. The American Robin behaves similarly when it is eating.

orange or yellow legs

some webbing between toes

🐦 **Home** Lives near beaches, lakes, and rivers.

🎵 **Voice** Gives a clear, whistled *chee-wee, chur-wee, chu-weet,* or *tyoo-eep.*

🌑 **Food** Along the sea coast it eats small shellfish and the eggs of marine animals. Inland it eats a lot of grasshoppers.

7.25 inches

Charadrius vociferus

Killdeer

The Killdeer is named for its loud cry, which can sound like *kill-deear*. It is the only plover in its range that has two bands across its chest. The Killdeer is one of many shorebirds that perform the "crippled bird act" if their nests or young are threatened.

gray-brown head and back

orange eye ring

bright reddish orange rump

thin black bill

The bird calls rapidly, drags its wings, spreads its tail, and even limps to one side to distract the intruder. When the intruder has left the area, the bird is "healed" and flies away.

white belly and chest

two black bands across chest

creamy pink legs and feet

🧗 **Home** Lives along river banks and near golf courses, fields, and neighborhood lawns.

🎵 **Voice** Loud cry sounds like *kill-deear* or *kill-deeah-dee-dee*. Also makes a long, trilled *trrrrrrrr* during its "crippled bird act."

🐦 **Food** Runs, stops, and stands still, then stabs at the ground with its bill to catch insects.

9–10.5 inches

American Oystercatcher

True to its name, the oystercatcher does eat oysters. The sharp tip of an oystercatcher's strong, flat bill is shaped like a chisel for prying open the oyster shells. The bill is more than twice as long as the bird's head.

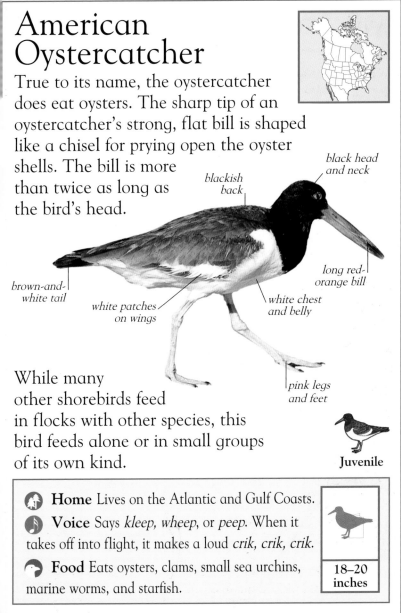

black head and neck

blackish back

brown-and-white tail

white patches on wings

long red-orange bill

white chest and belly

pink legs and feet

Juvenile

While many other shorebirds feed in flocks with other species, this bird feeds alone or in small groups of its own kind.

🌲 **Home** Lives on the Atlantic and Gulf Coasts.

🎵 **Voice** Says *kleep, wheep,* or *peep.* When it takes off into flight, it makes a loud *crik, crik, crik.*

🐦 **Food** Eats oysters, clams, small sea urchins, marine worms, and starfish.

18–20 inches

American Avocet

The avocet sweeps its long bill back and forth in shallow water to stir up its food. The bird keeps its bill partly open to filter the food from the water. Avocets feed in flocks. You might see these birds walking shoulder to shoulder with their bills in the water, all moving their heads back and forth at the same time.

In deeper water they feed like ducks by tipping over into the water bill-first.

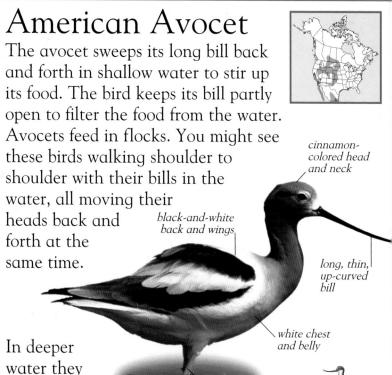

cinnamon-colored head and neck

black-and-white back and wings

long, thin, up-curved bill

white chest and belly

long blue-gray legs

Winter adult

🏠 **Home** In summer lives near lakes and rivers, and sometimes grasslands. In winter lives at the seashore, in marshes, ponds, and lakes.

🎵 **Voice** Loudly calls *wheet* or *pleeet*.

🐟 **Food** Eats water insects as well as shrimp and other crustaceans.

18–20 inches

Greater Yellowlegs

When it is frightened, the Greater
Yellowlegs whistles a loud alarm call.
Other shorebirds respond to this
alarm as a warning. This gray
sandpiper can be identified by
its large size, white tail,
and long bright-
yellow legs.

long grayish bill

dark gray-brown back with white speckles

long, slender neck

white breast and belly with brown speckles and bars

A similar bird, the
Lesser Yellowlegs,
is smaller and
thinner and has
a straighter and
shorter bill.

long bright-yellow legs

🌲 **Home** Lives in open marshes and near ponds,
streams, or flooded fields and golf courses.

🎵 **Voice** Makes a loud, repeated *teu-teu-teu*
that goes down in pitch. Also sings *too-whee* to let
other birds know about its territory.

🦅 **Food** Eats small fish, insects, crabs, and snails.

14 inches

Catoptrophorus semipalmatus

Willet

The best way to identify this member of the sandpiper family is by the black-and-white pattern on its wings. You might see this bird standing on one leg, sleeping with its head tucked into the feathers on its back. Near its nesting area the Willet sometimes perches high on rocks, posts, or other tall objects so it can look for intruders.

white ring around eyes goes to bill

bold black-and-white pattern on wings

blue-gray legs and feet

Winter adult

🌲 **Home** Lives on sandy seashore or in freshwater marshes.

🎵 **Voice** Calls *pill-will-will; pill-o-will-o-willet;* or *pill-will-willet.* When disturbed by an intruder, it calls *kip* or *wiek.* Calls out *wee-wee-weet* in flight.

🐦 **Food** In the water it eats insects, marine worms, crabs, mollusks, and small fish. On land it eats seeds, tender young plants, and rice.

13–16 inches

Spotted Sandpiper

This is the most widespread sandpiper in North America. In spring and summer you can identify it by its spotted white breast. In fall and winter this bird loses its spots. Watch for the Spotted Sandpiper's habit of bobbing its tail up and down as it walks.

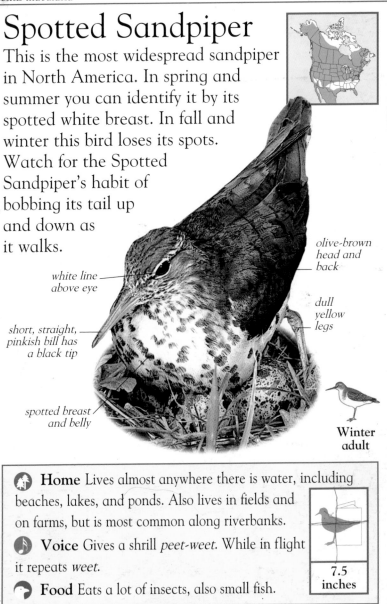

white line above eye

olive-brown head and back

short, straight, pinkish bill has a black tip

dull yellow legs

spotted breast and belly

Winter adult

Home Lives almost anywhere there is water, including beaches, lakes, and ponds. Also lives in fields and on farms, but is most common along riverbanks.

Voice Gives a shrill *peet-weet*. While in flight it repeats *weet*.

Food Eats a lot of insects, also small fish.

7.5 inches

Ruddy Turnstone

The turnstone is named for the way it searches for food. Using its short, pointed bill, this sandpiper flips over stones, shells, and seaweed on the shore to eat the small creatures hiding underneath. You also might see it cleaning up leftovers from beach picnics.

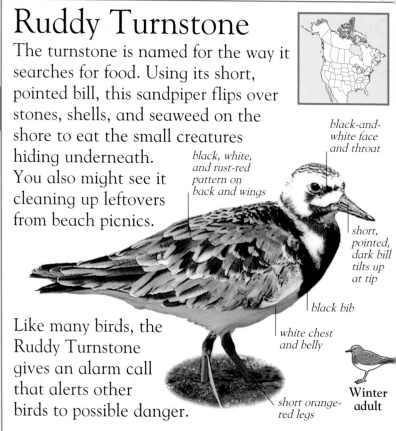

black, white, and rust-red pattern on back and wings

black-and-white face and throat

short, pointed, dark bill tilts up at tip

black bib

white chest and belly

short orange-red legs

Like many birds, the Ruddy Turnstone gives an alarm call that alerts other birds to possible danger.

Winter adult

🐦 **Home** Lives on the coast and around the Great Lakes except while it is breeding on the arctic tundra.

🎵 **Voice** Alarm call is *chick-ik* or *kewk*. In flight, it says *ket-ah-kek* or *kit-it-it*.

🌑 **Food** Eats insects, mollusks, crustaceans and their eggs, worms, and bird eggs. Sometimes eats the leftovers of other birds such as oystercatchers.

9–10 inches

Sanderling

You can see this little bird on the beach, running back and forth as the waves wash up onto the sand and back down. As the water moves off the sand, it exposes sand crabs, which are what the Sanderling mostly eats. When not hunting for food, this sandpiper stands on the beach away from the water. It often will stand on one leg with its head tucked into its back.

Juvenile

rust-colored wash on head, breast, and back

black bill

white belly

black legs and feet

has no hind toe

Winter adult

🌐 **Home** Lives on rocky or sandy seashores and nests on the stony tundra of the Far North.

🎵 **Voice** Gives a harsh *kree*. In flight it cries *twick* or *kip*.

🦐 **Food** Eats sand crabs and other crustaceans, mollusks, marine worms, and insects.

8 inches

Least Sandpiper

Tiny sandpipers such as this one are known as "peeps." This is the smallest sandpiper in North America, and one of the smallest shorebirds in the world. It gathers in flocks that fly together in unison, wheeling, banking, and twisting.

brownish gray head and back

thin, dark bi curves down slightly

white belly

pale green-yellow legs

streaked neck and breast

There are other, more common sandpipers along the coast, but inland this is the one you are most likely to see. It is the only peep with yellow legs.

Winter adult

🌲 **Home** Lives in wetland habitats and along the muddy shores of rivers and ponds.

🎵 **Voice** Gives a high *kneet* or *knee-eet*.

🐦 **Food** Picks small animals from the surface of mud and probes in the mud with its bill for insects, insect larvae, and small crustaceans.

6 inches

Common Snipe

This sandpiper has a long bill
designed to capture prey
underground. The bill can bend,
which helps the bird feel and
catch its prey in the soft
mud. The snipe's bill is
twice the length of its
head. When surprised,
a snipe bursts up
and flies in a
zigzag path.
Then it dives
straight
back to
the ground.

eyes set far back on face

distinctly striped head and back

long, thin bill

greenish legs and feet

🐦 **Home** Found near marshes and other wet areas.
Nests on the ground.

🎵 **Voice** Makes a scratchy *zhak* call after being
surprised and flying into the air. Says *wheat-wheat-wheat* on breeding grounds.

🐛 **Food** Eats worms, insects, and tender roots
found in mud and soft dirt.

10–11 inches

Laughing Gull

This gull was named for its laughlike call. It will sometimes catch food thrown in the air by people. The Laughing Gull has been known to steal food right out of the Brown Pelican's pouch.

black head

red bill

dark-gray wings and back

Juvenile

white breast

dark legs

First Winter

Thousands nest together in colonies. In winter, the Laughing Gull's head turns mostly white.

Second Winter

🏠 **Home** Lives along beaches, salt marshes, and bays.

🎵 **Voice** Long, loud call of *ha-ha-ha-hah-ha-ha*.

🐦 **Food** Does not dive, but snatches food from the surface of the water or ground. Eats scraps left by people. Also eats fish, crabs, insects, and other small animals. Will steal food from other birds.

15–17 inches

Ring-billed Gull

One of the most common gulls in North America, this crow-sized bird has adapted well to living near people. It will eat just about anything. It follows plows to find bugs and worms and will steal food from other birds.

yellow bill with black ring

white face and breast

pale-gray back and upper wings

greenish yellow legs and feet

It even searches through garbage dumps and begs for food in parking lots. It takes a young bird three years to look like an adult.

Juvenile

First Winter

Second Winter

Third Winter

🏠 **Home** Found on beaches and inland in fields and on lakes.

🎵 **Voice** Makes a shrill *ky-ow* or high-pitched *hiyak, hiyak.*

🍎 **Food** Eats worms, insects, and other small animals, as well as grain and garbage.

18–19 inches

Larus argentatu

Herring Gull

This large gull likes to soar high overhead like a hawk. It prefers to nest on the ground, but if people move into its area, it will nest in trees or on roofs. Like other gulls, this bird sometimes will drop clams and other shellfish from the air to break open the shells. Young birds take four years to look like adults.

white head and breast

yellow bill with red spot

black wing tips

light-gray wings and back

pinkish legs and feet

Second Winter

Third Winter

Dark Juvenile

Fourth Winter

Home Common along the coasts, especially in harbors and at garbage dumps. Also lives on rivers and lakes.

Voice Has several noisy calls, including *yucka-yucka-yucka*, *kek-kek-kek*, and a trumpetlike *kee-ow, kee-ou*.

Food Eats fish, worms, insects, and other small animals, as well as berries and garbage.

22–26 inches

Great Black-backed Gull

North America's largest gull will attack and eat almost any animal that is smaller than itself. However, it is shier around people than most gulls. This gull flies with slow wing beats. It sails in circles, high in the sky, like a hawk. A young bird takes three years to look like an adult.

white head and breast

yellow bill with red spot

black wings and back

Juvenile

Second Winter

white belly

pinkish legs

Third Winter

🏠 **Home** Lives along beaches and in lagoons. Can be found at garbage dumps. Nests on islands in colonies with Herring Gulls.

🎵 **Voice** Makes a low *keeow, keeow*.

🦅 **Food** Eats eggs, fish, shellfish, small birds, and other small animals. Also eats dead animals and scraps left by people.

28–31 inches

Sterna hirun

Common Tern

In some places along the coast of North America this is the most common tern. It flies over open water searching for food. After spotting a meal, it will dive straight into the water. Fishermen often follow this bird to find the best spots to fish. It is sometimes called the Mackerel Gull or Lake Erie Gull.

Juvenile

First Summer

pale gray wings and back

black cap

red bill with black tip

red legs and feet

forked tail

🏠 **Home** Lives along beaches, lakes, and rivers.

🎵 **Voice** Makes a low, piercing *kee-ar-r-r-r*. Also gives a high-pitched *kik-kik-kik*.

🦅 **Food** Dives for and eats mostly small fish, but also some crustaceans.

13–16 inches

Forster's Tern

Like other terns, this bird feeds while flying. It will scoop fish from the surface of the water or dive to catch a meal. Because it prefers to live in marshes, some people call it the Marsh Tern. In winter, the bird's head turns white and the black cap is replaced with a narrow black eye patch.

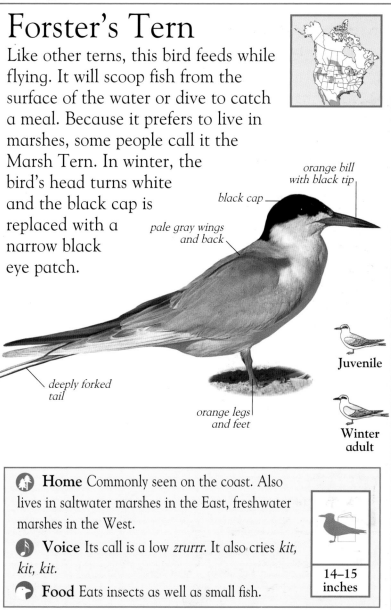

orange bill with black tip

black cap

pale gray wings and back

deeply forked tail

orange legs and feet

Juvenile

Winter adult

🏠 **Home** Commonly seen on the coast. Also lives in saltwater marshes in the East, freshwater marshes in the West.

🎵 **Voice** Its call is a low *zrurrr*. It also cries *kit, kit, kit.*

🌰 **Food** Eats insects as well as small fish.

14–15 inches

Black Guillemot

This hardy bird spends all of its time
in the North, even in sub-zero
weather. In winter, most of the
black feathers turn white or
gray. It nests in holes and
cracks on sea cliffs or on
rock piles in large colonies.
Unlike other members of
its family, this sea bird
can often be seen
close to shore.

narrow,
pointed
bill

solid black
body

large white
wing patch

bright-red feet
and legs

**Winter
adult**

🌳 **Home** Lives along rocky northern coasts.

🎵 **Voice** Makes a sound like a squeaky toy.

🐟 **Food** Dives as deep as 100 feet below the
surface to catch fish and other small sea creatures,
especially eels. The bird uses its wings to swim,
which makes it look like it is "flying" underwater.

12–14
inches

Atlantic Puffin

Puffins spend most of their time at
sea, using their strong wings to fly
in the air and swim underwater.
They build their nests
in tunnels, called
burrows, on the
rocky shore.
Sometimes
a pair of
puffins will
tap their bills
together,
rapidly swinging
their heads from
side to side. The
Atlantic Puffin is
the official bird of
Newfoundland and
Labrador.

white face

black
back

Juvenile

thick orange,
yellow, and
blue-black bill

white
breast and
belly

orange feet
and legs

**Winter
adult**

🏠 **Home** Stays on the ocean most of the year.
Colonies nest in burrows on rocky coasts.

🎵 **Voice** Makes a purring sound in flight. Near
the nest it makes a croaking *arrrr* sound.

🐟 **Food** Eats mostly fish. Also likes other sea
creatures such as squid and worms.

12 inches

Phasianus colchicus

Ring-necked Pheasant

The colorful male is easy to spot. The female is mostly brown, so she is better at concealing herself. A pheasant sometimes makes a loud whirring sound when it is flying. It usually flies only a short distance, then lands and runs away. The Ring-necked Pheasant is not native to North America – people brought this bird here from Asia. It is the state bird of South Dakota.

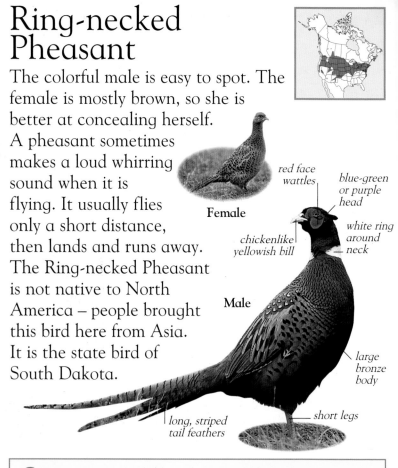

Female

red face
wattles

blue-green
or purple
head

white ring
around
neck

chickenlike
yellowish bill

Male

large
bronze
body

long, striped
tail feathers

short legs

Home Lives in fields and open woods.

Voice Clucks like a chicken. Male also makes a loud *KOCK-cack* call, like a rooster.

Food Eats mostly seeds, grains, and berries. Also eats large insects, such as grasshoppers, as well as mice and snails.

21–36 inches

Willow Ptarmigan

In winter this bird turns white except for its black tail. This helps it hide in the snow. In summer the male is rusty-red, and the female is brown. This helps the birds hide against dark rocks. The feathers on the Willow Ptarmigan's legs and toes act like snowshoes. Male birds stand guard while the females sit on their eggs. This is the state bird of Alaska.

no red eyebrows

gray-brown body

Female

red eyebrows can be hidden

stout black bill

Male

square tail

feathered legs and toes

Winter adult

🏠 **Home** Lives in the arctic tundra. Likes areas with willows and bushes.

🎵 **Voice** During mating season, males bark *go-back, go-back, go-back.*

🐦 **Food** Eats some insects, but mostly tender leaves, buds, and flowers. It especially likes willows.

15–17 inches

Meleagris gallopav

Wild Turkey

American colonists enjoyed turkey at the first Thanksgiving feast. Even before then, the turkey was a popular game bird. It seldom flies far and prefers to run from danger. Males are called "gobblers" or "toms." Females are called "jennies." Wild Turkeys roost in trees at night.

fanlike tail

naked blue-and-pink head

red wattle

smaller head

large, shiny, bronze body

usually has no beard

black beard

pink legs

smaller body is duller in color

Female

Male

🏠 **Home** Lives in forests with fields nearby.

🎵 **Voice** Male gobbles. Males and females make *cluk, cluk, cluk* sounds.

🪶 **Food** Eats acorns, seeds, nuts, and berries, as well as insects.

37–46 inches

Northern Bobwhite

The name of this bird comes from the clear call of the male: *bob-WHITE, bob-bob-WHITE.*
The bobwhite is a type of quail. A group of quail is called a covey. Like other quail, bobwhites explode into flight when surprised. A covey of these birds sleeps together on the ground. They put their tails together and face outward, like a wagon wheel. They sometimes can be seen running along the ground.

white stripe over eyes

reddish brown body

white throat

Male

short gray tail

cream stripe over eyes

short, dark bill

buff throat

Female

Home Lives in farmlands, grasslands, open forests, and open country.

Voice Clearly whistles its name *bob-WHITE, bob-bob-WHITE.*

Food Eats mostly seeds, but also fruit and insects. Visits ground feeders for mixed seed.

9–10 inches

Columba livi

Rock Dove

Some of the fastest birds in flight, Rock Doves have been used to carry messages. They are different from most birds because they come in different colors. One might be brown, gray, white, or a combination of those colors.

neck feathers shine green, bronze, or purple

short curved bill

blue-gray overall

You will see them in parks and parking lots, on telephone wires, and in many other places near people. The Rock Dove is not native to North America – people brought this bird here from Asia.

Color variations

🐦 **Home** Lives in the city, nesting on buildings or under tall bridges. Likes rocky areas in the wild.

🎵 **Voice** Softly sings, *coo-a-roo, coo-roo-coo.*

🌰 **Food** Eats grass, seeds, and berries in the wild. Likes bread crumbs and other scraps in the city.

13–14 inches

Mourning Dove

This is the most common dove
in neighborhoods
and farmyards.
Its wings
make a
whistling
sound when it
flies. It feeds
mostly on the
ground. Male
and female
share the job of
sitting on eggs.
Young doves, called
squabs, are fed
"pigeon milk," which is
made in the crops of both
male and female adult birds.
The crop is a special food storage
organ in the neck of the bird.

black spot
on lower
cheek

Juvenile

black spots
on wings

brownish
gray body

pink legs
and feet

long dark tail
with white
edges and tip

🌲 **Home** Lives in cities and towns, as well as in
the open countryside.

🎵 **Voice** Makes a sad-sounding *coo-ooh, coo,
coo-coo.*

🐚 **Food** Eats seeds, grains, berries, and insects.

12 inches

Turkey Vulture

When flying, this bird's wings are
held up in an angle, not straight
across like some other vultures.
Groups of vultures soar
in circles in the sky.
The similar Black
Vulture is smaller
and has a
black head.

small, bald,
red head

light bill

large brown-
black body

yellow legs
and feet

The vulture's strong sense
of smell helps it find food.
This bird is helpful because
it gets rid of dead animals.
The Cherokee call the
Turkey Vulture the Peace Eagle
because it rarely kills anything.

Juvenile

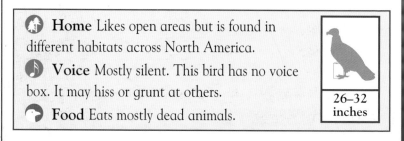

🌲 **Home** Likes open areas but is found in
different habitats across North America.

🎵 **Voice** Mostly silent. This bird has no voice
box. It may hiss or grunt at others.

🍖 **Food** Eats mostly dead animals.

26–32
inches

Osprey

Also called the "fish hawk," this bird dives into the water feet first to catch fish. It can dive from as high as 100 feet above the water. An Osprey has sharp, curved claws to help it hold slippery fish, which it usually carries head first into the wind as it flies. This is the official bird of Nova Scotia.

mostly white head

white belly

long tail with thin black bands

sharp, curved claws

Juvenile

🏠 **Home** One of the most widespread birds in the world, it is found on every continent except Antarctica. Lives near coasts, rivers, and lakes. Often seen perching on a dead tree branch or on large rocks.

🎵 **Voice** Its loud whistles sound like *kyew* or *chewk-chewk-chewk*.

🔴 **Food** Eats fish. On rare occasions it will eat small mammals, birds, or reptiles.

21–24 inches

Elanoides forficatus

Swallow-tailed Kite

The black-and-white pattern on this bird is hard to mistake. The kite is a graceful flyer, and you are most likely to see one flying high in the air. The forked tail of a Swallow-tailed Kite is a little longer than 12 inches. It opens and closes like scissors to help the bird turn. The kite catches most of its food while flying. It will fly low and skim water in an open field to take a drink and bathe.

white head

small black bill

black flight feathers

white wing linings

white belly and breast

long, forked black tail

🌲 **Home** Prefers swampy forests with nearby grasslands. Also lives in marshes, swamps, and pine woods.

🎵 **Voice** Normally silent but has a high-pitched alarm call, *klee, klee, klee.*

🐦 **Food** Eats mostly insects. Plucks fruit. Also eats lizards, frogs, small birds, and bird eggs.

19–25 inches

Bald Eagle

This awesome bird, which lives only in North America, is the US national bird. Although it is known for its white head and tail, young birds, or juveniles, are mostly brown until they are four or five years old. Nesting Bald Eagles add a new layer of loose sticks to the same nest each year. A nest can grow to the size of a king-size bed.

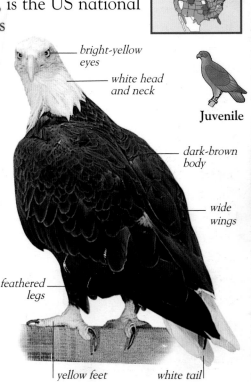

bright-yellow eyes

white head and neck

Juvenile

dark-brown body

wide wings

feathered legs

yellow feet

white tail

🏞 **Home** Lives on the coast and near large lakes and rivers.

🎵 **Voice** Has a squeaky cackle, *kleek-kik-ik-ik-ik* or a lower *kak-kak-kak*.

🦅 **Food** Catches fish with its talons and will eat small mammals and waterfowl. Will steal food from other birds. Also eats dead animals.

34–43 inches

Circus cyaneus

Northern Harrier

Unlike some hawks that hunt high in the sky, the Northern Harrier flies close to the ground and uses its keen sense of hearing to take prey by surprise. In flight this bird shows a white patch of feathers on its back just above the tail, called a rump patch. A harrier often flies with its wings held above its body, which makes the bird look like a shallow V.

gray head and back

Male

gray breast

black wing tips

brown head and back

white belly

Female **Juvenile**

very long tail

🌲 **Home** Formerly called the Marsh Hawk, this bird lives near marshes and wet meadows, as well as on open grasslands.

🎵 **Voice** Usually silent. You might hear a shrill *kee-kee-kee* when it is near its nest.

🐦 **Food** Eats mainly mice, rats, frogs, and snakes but also eats lizards, crayfish, insects, birds, and dead animals.

16–24 inches

Sharp-shinned Hawk

small head

blue-gray back

red-brown bars on chest and belly

Up close, you can see that the Sharp-shinned Hawk's legs are slightly flat, giving them a sharp edge on the front. This is how the bird got its name. As it flies, you can see the wings are short and rounded, and the tail looks square. This shape lets the hawk fly fast and make quick, sharp turns, which helps as it chases other birds.

pencil-like bright-yellow legs

Juvenile

long tail with bold stripes

🐦 **Home** Lives in forests. Nests in conifer trees. Can be seen just about anywhere during migration.

🎵 **Voice** When it is alarmed, this hawk cackles *kek-kek-kek*. Its call is a sad-sounding cry.

🦅 **Food** Eats mostly other birds. It will attack prey in the air, on the ground, or in trees. Also eats mice, shrews, bats, frogs, lizards, and insects.

10–14 inches

Buteo jamaicensis

Red-tailed Hawk

This is one of the most common hawks in North America. When it flies, the adult's rust-red, fan-shaped tail makes the bird easy to identify. You are likely to see this bird along a road looking for prey.

rust-red tail

There are five races of this bird that are different colors. One that lives in the Great Plains, called Krider's Red-tailed Hawk, has a pink tail.

large bill

white belly with broad band of dark streaking

Krider's Red-tailed

🏠 **Home** Prefers a mix of open areas and trees. Lives across North America, except on the tundra and deep in forests.

🎵 **Voice** Cry sounds like a squealing pig, *kree-kree ree-e-e-e.*

🔴 **Food** Swoops down to catch mice, rats, squirrels, rabbits, prairie dogs, and other small birds, snakes, lizards, frogs, and insects.

19–25 inches

American Kestrel

This is the smallest and most
common falcon in North
America. The
female, which
has a brown back
and wings, is not as
brightly colored as
the male. The kestrel
can often be seen
perched on utility
wires, bobbing its
tail as it looks for
prey on the ground.
If it spots a meal it
often stops in midair
to hover before
swooping down to
make the catch.

*light breast
and belly
with streaks*

*reddish tail
with black
stripes*

Female

*two dark
lines come
down
from eyes*

*reddish
back with
dark bars*

*blue-gray
wings*

*spotted
tan
breast*

Male

*reddish tail has
white tips and one
wide black band*

🐦 **Home** Lives at the edge of woods, in open fields, along
highways, in wooded canyons, and on plains and deserts.
Takes over nesting holes other birds have made.

🎵 **Voice** Because this bird says *killy-killy-killy*,
some people call it a Killy Hawk.

🌑 **Food** Eats insects, mice, bats, birds, lizards,
small snakes, frogs, and other small animals.

**9–12
inches**

Falco peregrinu

Peregrine Falcon

One of the fastest birds in the world, the Peregrine Falcon can fly 175 miles per hour. At one time there were few of these birds left in the United States. Pesticides were preventing the falcon from hatching and raising its young. Because these chemicals make the eggshells thin, the eggs often do not hatch. Now that people are using less of these poison chemicals, more birds are hatching and surviving.

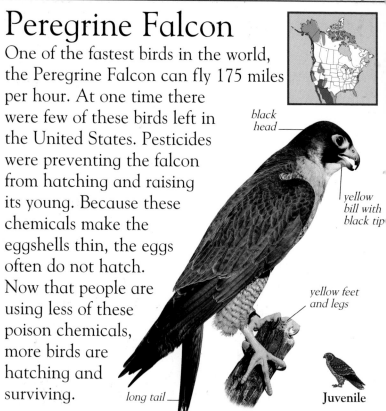

black head

yellow bill with black tip

yellow feet and legs

long tail

Juvenile

🌲 **Home** Nests on cliffs. Also lives on buildings in large cities. Flies south in winter but returns to the same nest each year. Some families have used the same nest for hundreds of years.

🎵 **Voice** Usually quiet. Near the nest it says *witchew, witchew, witchew.*

🐦 **Food** Eats other birds. Flies high above its prey, then dives down to catch it in the air.

16–20 inches

Barn Owl

The heart-shaped "monkey" face and long legs make this owl easy to identify. The well-named Barn Owl is often found in barns, where there are plenty of mice to eat. Like most other owls, this bird hunts at night and sleeps during the day. Although the disks on its face are a different shape from those of other owls, they do the same thing. The disks collect sound waves to help the owl hear better.

dark eyes

no ear tufts

heart-shaped disks on face

long legs

Home Lives in the forest and in open fields. Makes its nest in a tree cavity, building, or cave. Some will use a nest box that people make for them.

Voice Makes a harsh, hissing screech that sounds like *eeeeeeSEEek.*

Food Eats small mammals, such as rodents and shrews. Also eats small birds.

14–20 inches

Otus asio

Eastern Screech-Owl

You will probably hear its whistling call more often than you will see this bird. Screech-Owls are nocturnal – they hunt at night. During the day they sleep huddled close to a tree trunk or in a hole in a tree. The pattern on their feathers serves as camouflage. You might see it in two different colors, or morphs.

ear tufts

yellow eyes

light-greenish bill

rusty-brown to gray body

heavily streaked breast and belly

Red Morph

gray body

white spots on wing

Gray Morph

🏠 **Home** Lives in many places, including wooded lots and neighborhood gardens.

🎵 **Voice** Males and females sing duets. The male's call sounds like a horse's whinny, and the female follows with a long trill.

🦉 **Food** Hunts at night for small animals such as mice, frogs, snakes, fish, birds, and insects.

8–10 inches

Bubo virginianus

Great Horned Owl

This is the most widespread and best-known owl in North America. It is a powerful hunter that will attack animals bigger than itself, even a cat or a dog. Like most owls, the Great Horned is mostly nocturnal, and its wings make no noise when it flies. This is the official bird of Alberta.

yellow eyes

feathers around ears look like horns

rusty patches on face with black edges

barred, brownish gray body

🐦 **Home** Lives in many places, including woods, marshes, mountains, and deserts.

🎵 **Voice** A series of three to eight soft, deep hoots, *Whoo! Whoo-whoo-whoo! Who! Who!* It sounds like "You awake? Me too!" Males and females sometimes sing together.

🔴 **Food** Grabs animals of all kinds with its talons, including mice, rabbits, foxes, skunks, birds, frogs, fish, insects, and even porcupines.

18–25 inches

Snowy Owl

True to its name, which refers to its white coloring, this owl lives in the snowy Far North. Unlike most owls, it is active day and night and nests on the ground. Its flight is smooth and strong, and it often glides in the air. If there is a shortage of its food, small animals called lemmings, it may go as far south as the United States. This is the official bird of Quebec.

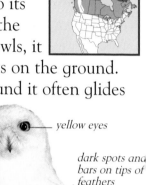

yellow eyes

dark spots and bars on tips of feathers

large round head

Male

Female

more dark bars than on male

all-white body

🏠 **Home** Nests in the arctic tundra. Spends winters along sea coasts, marshes, meadows, lakes, and rivers.

🎵 **Voice** Usually silent. Near its breeding grounds it makes a loud, growling bark, *krow-ow*, or a sharp whistle.

🌐 **Food** Lemmings and mice are its main foods. Also hunts other small mammals, birds, and fish.

20–24 inches

Barred Owl

This "hoot owl" is common in wet woodlands and swamps in the South. It is active mostly at night, but it can often be heard in the daytime. If you imitate its call, this owl might answer. Sometimes it will come closer if you make squeaky mouse sounds and stay very still. This owl generally keeps the same mate for life and uses the same nesting site for many years.

large, round head

brown back and wings with white spots

dark eyes

horizontal bars on upper breast

vertical streaks on lower breast

long tail with barred markings

🏠 **Home** Common in swamps and along rivers in the South. Also found in woodlands in the North.

🎵 **Voice** Usually hoots eight times in a row. (That is why it is also called a "hoot owl.") Sounds like "Who cooks for you; who cooks for you-all?"

🦅 **Food** Hunts mostly mice and small mammals. Also eats birds, salamanders, and insects.

17–24 inches

Common Nighthawk

Nighthawks are often seen at dusk, flying around street lights to catch insects. When a male is courting a female, he makes big swooping dives in the air. At the bottom of the dive his wings make a sound like a rubber band being plucked.

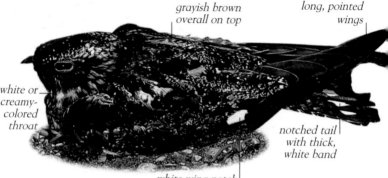

grayish brown overall on top

long, pointed wings

white or creamy-colored throat

notched tail with thick, white band

white wing patch

The nighthawk has coloring that blends with its surroundings, which makes it nearly impossible to see while it is sitting on its nest on the ground.

Home Lives in different habitats across North America – in city and country, woodlands and fields.

Voice Has a froglike call of *peeant* or *beant*. You might hear this bird before you see it.

Food Commonly seen flying around lights at night as it catches huge amounts of insects.

8–10 inches

Whip-poor-will

The Whip-poor-will, which is heard
more often than it is seen, blends in
completely with the branches or
ground on which it sits. While most
birds perch sideways on a
branch, the Whip-
poor-will, like   *spotted*
                   brownish
other members   *body*
of the nightjar
family, lies

large eyes

*short
bill*

*long tail with
cream-colored tips*

lengthwise on a branch. Sometimes the bird is
spotted sitting beside country roads at night
when car lights cause a red reflection in its eyes.

Home Lives on farmlands, in woods, and near fields.

Voice A loud clear *whip-poor-will* repeated at
night. Southwestern birds have a call that is
coarser than that of eastern birds.

Food Flies low at night to catch insects such
as moths, beetles, crickets, and mosquitoes.

9–10
inches

Chimney Swift

Commonly seen in a flock of twittering, fluttering birds at sunset, this is the only swift you are likely to see in eastern North America. This bird looks like a "flying cigar." Entire colonies will nest in a single tall chimney, which is how the bird was named. Stiff spines on the end of the short tail help the swift hold onto bricks. It builds a cup-shaped nest of sticks, using its sticky saliva to glue the nest to the wall of the chimney.

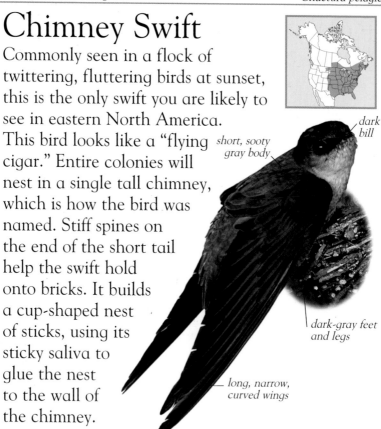

dark bill

short, sooty gray body

dark-gray feet and legs

long, narrow, curved wings

🏠 **Home** Well adapted to life around people, it roosts and nests in chimneys, airshafts, and barns. Likes hollow trees in the wild.

🎵 **Voice** Bold chattering and rapid twittering.

🐦 **Food** Catches insects while flying, including beetles, mosquitoes, flies, ants, and termites. Also eats young spiders that "balloon" through the air.

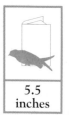

5.5 inches

Ruby-throated Hummingbird

Like a lot of other hummingbirds, this glittery green bird seems to love the color red. This "hummer" can beat its wings very fast, up to 75 times per second. Listen carefully and you will hear the humming noise the wings make. This is the only hummingbird that nests east of the Mississippi River.

green head

glittery green

black face

red throat

Male

Female

🏠 **Home** Lives in forests and near the forest edge. Also visits gardens and backyards.

🎵 **Voice** Makes fast, squeaky *chip chip chip*.

🍴 **Food** Drinks nectar from many kinds of flowers. Also eats many insects, particularly ants. Attracted to the color red. Visits hummingbird feeders for sugar water. But do not color the water red because it can make them sick.

3 inches

Red-headed Woodpecker

Like most woodpeckers, the Red-headed eats insects found in trees, but it sometimes will fly out to catch a passing insect. It stores extra acorns and nuts for the winter. The male uses his powerful bill to drill a hole for its nest. This is the only woodpecker in the East with a solid-red head.

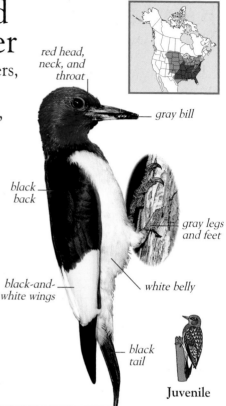

red head, neck, and throat

gray bill

black back

gray legs and feet

black-and-white wings

white belly

black tail

Juvenile

🏠 **Home** Likes farms, golf courses, open woodlands, and other open areas. Some will nest in birdhouses for woodpeckers.

🎵 **Voice** Fairly noisy. Makes a bold *queark*, or *queer, queer, queer* call in the breeding season. Also makes a sound like a chicken clucking, *kerr-uck, kerr-uck*.

🐛 **Food** Eats mostly insects, spiders, millipedes, and centipedes. Visits feeders for suet, sunflower seeds, cracked corn, raisins, nuts, and bread.

8.5–9.25 inches

Red-bellied Woodpecker

The hint of red on this bird's belly is difficult to see. What you will see is the red on its crown and down the nape, or back of its neck. Like other woodpeckers, the Red-bellied has a stiff tail that it uses to brace itself while hanging on the side of a tree.

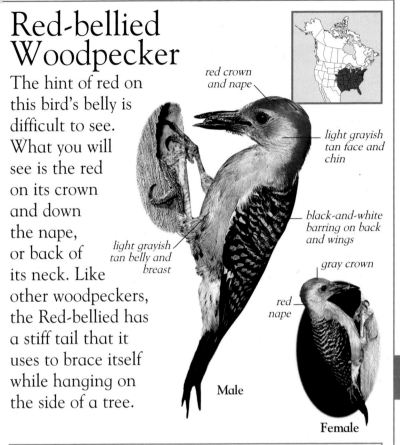

red crown and nape

light grayish tan face and chin

black-and-white barring on back and wings

light grayish tan belly and breast

gray crown

red nape

Male

Female

🏠 **Home** Lives in woods, swamps, and neighborhoods. Males stay in the breeding area all year.

🎵 **Voice** Noisy. Makes a shaky *churr-churr* or *querrr-querrr*. Also says *chuck, chuck, chuck*.

🐛 **Food** Eats insects, fruits, and berries. Visits birdfeeders for suet, peanut butter, nuts, and sunflower seeds.

9–10.5 inches

Yellow-bellied Sapsucker

Sapsuckers drill rows of holes in the trunks of trees. These holes are called "sap wells." The bird drinks the sap that collects in the wells. During the breeding season, male and female drum loudly together on dry limbs, tin roofs, or utility poles. They also use sharp, irregular tapping to communicate with each other. A female is similar to a male but she has a white throat.

red forehead and front of crown

red throat

Male

black-and-white face

white stripe on wing

pale yellowish belly

Juvenile

🐦 **Home** Lives in forests, yards, orchards, and parks.

🎵 **Voice** Often silent. Sounds somewhat like a cat, with a low *mew*. When alarmed says *cheee-er, cheeee-er*. During courtship, male and female cry *hoih-hoih*.

🐦 **Food** In addition to tree sap and bark, this bird eats insects that damage the tree. Also eats a lot of ants, as well as tree buds, fruits, and berries. Visits suet feeders in winter.

8–9 inches

Downy Woodpecker

This is the smallest woodpecker in North America. In the spring, the male and the female search together for a place to nest. After making a decision, they tap on the tree of their choice. Every fall, each bird digs a fresh hole in a dead tree, where it will roost. It takes five to eight days to dig a hole. The female looks like the male, except she does not have the red spot on the back of her head.

black crown

short black bill

red patch on back of head

black shoulders

white back

white belly

black wings with white spots

🏠 **Home** Lives almost anywhere there are trees, including suburbs and orchards. Will use a nest box designed for it.

🎵 **Voice** Makes a high-pitched but soft whinny, like a horse. Call is a flat *pik* or *pick*.

🐦 **Food** Digs insects and grubs from bark. Also eats caterpillars, spiders, snails, berries, and nuts. Visits feeders for suet, peanut butter, sunflower seeds, and bread.

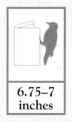

6.75–7 inches

Northern Flicker

This bird eats a lot of ants, perhaps more than any other bird in North America. There are two different kinds of Northern Flicker. The "yellow-shafted" bird is yellow beneath its wings and tail. Also called a "yellowhammer," this is the state bird of Alabama. The "red-shafted" is red beneath its wings and tail and has a red mustache. Both have a black crescent bib.

Red-shafted male

red crescent on back of head

brown back and wings with black bars

gray forehead

tan face

black mustache

black spots on pale chest and belly

Yellow-shafted male

🏠 **Home** Lives in woods, neighborhoods, and in the desert. The yellow-shafted bird lives in the East, Canada, and Alaska. The red-shafted bird lives in the West. These birds will nest in birdhouses and nest boxes.

🎵 **Voice** Loudly says *klee-yer* or *clearrrr* and *wicker, wicker, wicker.*

🍂 **Food** Eats mostly ants, often on the ground. Also eats other insects, fruits, and berries.

12.75–14 inches

Pileated Woodpecker

The largest woodpecker in North America drums on trees so loudly it might scare you. This loud drumming helps to establish territory and attract a mate. While looking for food, the Pileated Woodpecker peels large strips of bark off the trees and digs rectangular holes deep into the trunk.

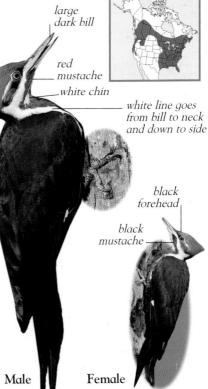

large dark bill

large red crest

red mustache

white chin

white line goes from bill to neck and down to side

black back

black forehead

black mustache

Male   **Female**

🏠 **Home** Lives in forests, swamps, woods, and even in cities. This bird is somewhat common in the Southeast.

🎵 **Voice** When calling its mate, it makes a loud *cuck, cuck, cuck.* Also says *yucka, yucka, yucka.*

🐦 **Food** Eats carpenter ants from trees and logs, as well as beetles, ants, and other insects. Also eats acorns, nuts, and fruits. Sometimes visits feeders for a mixture of suet, pecans, and walnuts.

16–20 inches

Yellow-billed Cuckoo

Cuckoos are shy, so they are hard to spot. They often sit perfectly still in trees and slip quietly through tangled bushes. They fly with deep "swimmer" strokes. You are most likely to see this bird when there is an outbreak of caterpillars, which are the cuckoo's favorite food.

grayish brown back

reddish wings

curved bill has yellow lower half

white breast and belly

gray feet and legs

white tips of tail feathers look like spots

Home Found in trees in thickets, orchards, overgrown pastures, and along country roadsides.

Voice Often silent, but sometimes sings *ka-ka-ka-ka-kow-kow-kow-kow-kowlp—kowlp——kowl*. The song slows down toward the end.

Food Loves caterpillars, plus other insects such as flies, beetles, wasps, grasshoppers, and tree crickets. Also eats fruits, lizards, and small frogs.

11–13 inches

Belted Kingfisher

Like other kingfishers, this bird has a bill and head that look too big for its body. The Belted Kingfisher is unusual among birds because the female is more colorful than the male. She has a reddish brown band across her belly, which the male does not have. A kingfisher dives headfirst into the water for its prey.

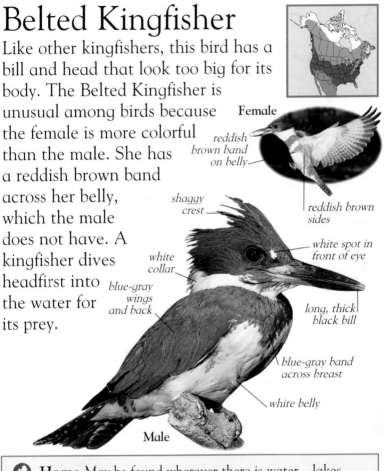

Female

reddish brown band on belly

reddish brown sides

white spot in front of eye

shaggy crest

white collar

blue-gray wings and back

long, thick black bill

blue-gray band across breast

white belly

Male

🏠 **Home** May be found wherever there is water – lakes, rivers, ponds, bays, mountain streams, and creeks.

🎵 **Voice** Makes bold, raspy rattle sounds, like a heavy fishing reel.

🐟 **Food** Eats mostly small fish. Also eats frogs, tadpoles, crayfish, small snakes, and insects.

11–14.5 inches

Least Flycatcher

large head

white eye ring

short bill

olive-green to brown back

light-gray breast

white wing bars

pale-yellow belly

This is the smallest eastern flycatcher. These birds often live together in loose groups, and their repeated *che-BECK* calls are easily heard. The Least Flycatcher sits silently on a tree branch, looking for insects. After spotting a meal, the bird flies up to grab its prey from a leaf.

🌲 **Home** Lives in woods and orchards. Can be found in trees along country roads and near water or fields.

🎵 **Voice** Repeats a hoarse *che-BECK*. Call is a sharp *whit*.

🦅 **Food** Eats many kinds of insects, including beetles, bees, treehoppers, leafhoppers, and especially ants. Even snatches insects from spider webs. Also eats elderberries and other small fruits.

5.25 inches

Eastern Phoebe

Phoebes, which are members of the flycatcher family, have a habit of wagging their tails up and down. The Eastern Phoebe is normally the only flycatcher that spends winter in the eastern United States. It is usually found near water and often builds its nest under bridges over streams. Its nest is made from bits of moss and mud and is lined with grass, leaves, hair, and feathers.

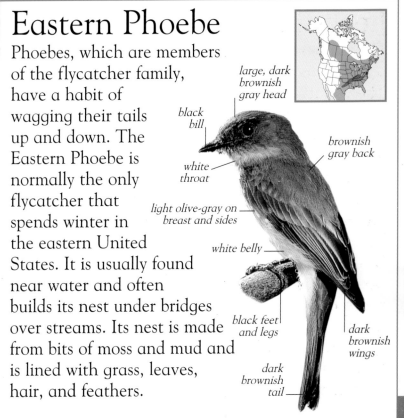

large, dark brownish gray head

black bill

white throat

brownish gray back

light olive-gray on breast and sides

white belly

black feet and legs

dark brownish wings

dark brownish tail

🏠 **Home** Lives in open woods near streams or other bodies of water.

🎵 **Voice** A sharp *chip* is the most common call. Also sings a grating *FEE-be*, which the bird often repeats many times as it sits on a perch.

🐦 **Food** Eats insects, including bees, wasps, flies, dragonflies, and crickets. Occasionally grabs small fish near the water's surface.

7 inches

Eastern Kingbird

The kingbird is part of the flycatcher family. This kingbird's scientific name means "king of the tyrants." The fearless little Eastern Kingbird is a tyrant because it will attack a hawk, a crow, or even a vulture for flying over its territory. On its black head is a red stripe that is usually hidden unless the bird raises the feathers on its head, which it does when defending its territory or trying to attract a female Eastern Kingbird.

black bill

black head has a hidden red stripe

white chin and throat

dark-gray back

pale-gray coloring on breast

white belly

black legs and feet

black tail ends with a white band

🏠 **Home** Found along roadsides; in parks, fields, and orchards; and on the edge of woods. Spends winter in South America.

🎵 **Voice** Makes a buzzing, high-pitched *dzeet*, combined with a rapid *tzi, tzeet, tzi, tzeet, tzi, tzeet.*

🦜 **Food** Catches insects in the air and on the ground. Also eats berries, fruits, and seeds.

8.5 inches

Loggerhead Shrike

Nicknamed the "Butcher Bird," this hunter perches on wires and fences to watch for a meal. From there, it swoops down and catches prey. Insects are the shrike's favorite food, but it might catch a small rodent, bird, or snake. The shrike has an unusual habit of sticking its prey on a sharp thorn or a barbed wire spike. Sometimes the bird tears its food apart there, and sometimes it saves the food for later.

large bluish gray head

hooked black beak

bluish gray back

black mask

black wings with white patch

Juvenile

black tail with white outer feathers

🏠 **Home** Lives in open areas along roadsides, orchards, grasslands, open woods, and hedges.

🎵 **Voice** Usually silent but makes a variety of squeaky notes and low warbles. Often repeats *queedle, queedle.* Its call is a grating *shak-shak.*

🐦 **Food** Eats small animals, including mice, small birds, insects, frogs, and snakes.

9 inches

Progne subi

Purple Martin

The largest member of the swallow family, the Purple Martin often nests in large colonies. Because martins eat a lot of insects, people like to attract these birds to their yards. If there is water nearby and plenty of open space for low flying, martins will move into the homes people make for them, such as groups of gourds with holes in them or birdhouses divided into apartments.

First Spring male

shiny dark purplish blue all over

blue-gray head, back, and wings

Male

gray to white lower breast and belly

forked bluish gray tail

Female

🏠 **Home** Lives in open areas near water. Nests in martin houses or in holes in tall dead trees. Winters in South America.

🎵 **Voice** Makes rich, low-pitched gurgling notes and chirping mixed with cackling.

🦅 **Food** Eats mostly insects it catches in the air such as dragonflies, mosquitoes, and moths.

7–9 inches

Tree Swallow

Swallows often migrate in big flocks. Many Tree Swallows spend the winter along the coast of the Gulf of Mexico and Florida. Because they will eat berries when they cannot find insects, some Tree Swallows stay farther north in winter than other types of swallows. Like other swallows, this bird's bill opens very wide. It acts as an insect trap while the bird flies through the air.

white cheek below eye

shiny dark greenish blue back, head, and wings

white breast and belly

slightly notched tail

Juvenile

🏠 **Home** Nests in holes in trees near water. Also nests in bird boxes or gourd houses and looks for food over fields.

🎵 **Voice** Gives a quick, repeating *silip* or *chi-veet*. When flying it sometimes makes a cheerful-sounding gurgling.

🐦 **Food** Catches insects, such as bees and flies, in the air. Stops on shore to eat sand fleas. Also eats spiders, seeds, and fruits.

5–6 inches

Hirundo rustica

Barn Swallow

Farmers welcome this bird because it eats insects that might destroy their crops. Like other swallows, the Barn Swallow feeds while in flight. A flock often nests together in a cave, under a bridge, or in a barn. That is how they got their name. This swallow is easy to tell apart from other swallows by its deeply forked tail and deep-blue back.

shiny blue-black neck, back, and top of wings

reddish brown forehead

reddish brown throat

chest and belly can be white or orange

long, deeply forked tail

Juvenile

Home Lives in open country. Often found nesting on farms, under bridges, and on cliffs along lakes.

Voice Repeats a short *chi-dit, chi-dit* or *wit-wit*. Its song is a long, twittering warble.

Food Catches insects in the air, such as dragonflies and moths. Follows farmers' plows to catch grasshoppers, crickets, and other insects.

6–8 inches

Blue Jay

Jays are in the crow family, which contains some of the boldest, noisiest birds in North America. Acting alone or in a group, the Blue Jay will shriek at cats, snakes, owls, hawks, and people that come into its territory. The Blue Jay once lived mainly in forests, but now this smart bird has adapted to living in cities. It often visits bird feeders for sunflower seeds, cracked nuts, corn, bread, or suet. This is the official bird of Prince Edward Island.

purplish crest and back

long black bill

black collar

white spots and black bars on blue wings

black bars on blue tail

🌲 **Home** Lives in oak forests, city parks, and yards.

🎵 **Voice** Call is a sharp *jay jay jay* or *thief, thief, thief!* Also has a musical *weedle, weedle*, like a squeaky farm pump that needs oil. Imitates several hawks.

🦜 **Food** Eats mostly acorns, nuts, corn, seeds, berries, and fruits. Also eats insects, snails, frogs, and other small animals.

11 inches

Corvus brachyrhynchos

American Crow

Simply called a crow by most people, this bird is one of the most widespread and well-known birds in North America. Family groups travel and feed together. Their diet includes a wide variety of food items. Crows are smart birds and are not fooled by scarecrows. Fearless and lively birds, they are often seen diving at hawks in the air. They like shiny things and may pick up a shiny object to take back to the nest.

brown eyes

black bill

solid black body

black legs and feet

short, fan-shaped tail

🏃 **Home** Lives wherever trees grow – in woods, on farms, and in neighborhoods.

🎵 **Voice** Most people know its loud *caw-caw*. It also has a begging call that sounds like *uh-uah*.

🐦 **Food** Eats animal and plant foods, including insects, spiders, snails, frogs, snakes, young birds and birds' eggs, worms, clams, dead animals, grains, fruits, and seeds.

17–18 inches

Blue-headed Vireo

This is one of the first vireos to return to eastern North America in the spring after spending the winter in the Southwest and in Central America. The Blue-headed Vireo is usually found alone or in pairs.

white ring around eye goes to bill

blue-gray head

white edges on tail

white breast, throat, and belly

bright-yellow sides

light bars on wing

This bird is not shy, but it feeds mostly in the treetops, so it can be hard to spot. When the male is courting a female, he fluffs out the yellow feathers on his sides. Then he bobs up and down and sings.

Home Lives in woods or in trees along streams.

Voice Slow song has stops between each phrase, *cherry-o-wit . . . cheree . . . sissy-a-wit.* The bird repeats this song all day. Also sings other high, clear, sweet notes. Call sounds like husky chatter.

Food Eats insects from twigs, branches, and leaves in trees. Also eats some fruits.

5.25 inches

Red-eyed Vireo

A Red-eyed Vireo may have set the record for being the longest-singing songbird. A single bird was recorded as singing an unbelievable 22,197 songs in 10 hours.

white eyebrow

blue-gray crown

olive-green back

red eye

darker wings and tail

heavy dark bill

white throat, breast, and belly

blue-gray legs and feet

This vireo almost never stops singing, and it is probably the most widespread forest bird in the East. If you make squeaking noises it often comes to see what is happening. Although this vireo is named for its red eye, young birds have brown eyes.

Home In summer, lives high in the tops of deciduous trees (lose their leaves in winter). Spends winter near the Amazon River in South America.

Voice Repeats this song, *look up! . . . see me? . . . over here . . . this way! . . . higher still!* Its call sounds like a whining, *chewy!*

Food Eats insects. Also likes dogwood berries and blackberries.

6 inches

Horned Lark

This songbird spends most of its time on the ground. However, the male performs a wonderful flight to impress a female. He flies high, then – while singing – he closes his wings and drops, headfirst, almost to the ground. At the last second he opens his wings to keep from crashing.

hornlike black tufts

white or yellowish face and throat

black mask

brown back and wings

black bib

white belly

black tail with white outer feathers

Then he perks up the hornlike feathers on his head, droops his wings, and struts around the female. Horned Larks form big flocks in winter.

🌳 **Home** Nests on the ground in open areas, such as fields, plains, tundra, airports, or beaches.

🎵 **Voice** Sings a series of bell-like, tinkling notes, *pit-wee, pit-wee*. Calls *tsee-tete* or *zeet*.

🦅 **Food** Runs or walks over the ground, eating seeds, grain, and insects such as grasshoppers.

7–8 inches

Carolina Chickadee

Put out sunflower seeds, and chickadees will come. Chickadees like to nest in a hole, so they will move into birdhouses. The Carolina and Black-capped Chickadees look a lot alike. They both have black caps and bibs.

white cheeks

black cap

gray back

small black bill

black bib

light breast and belly

However, Black-capped Chickadees generally stay farther north and west. A lively little bird, the Carolina Chickadee calls out its name as it darts from feeder to branch – *chick-a-dee-dee-dee.*

dark-gray legs and feet

Home Lives in woods and neighborhoods.

Voice Rapidly calls *chick-a-dee-dee-dee.* Also makes a variety of high, squeaky notes and gives a simple whistled *fee-bee-fee-by.*

Food Eats moths and other insects. In winter, eats mostly seeds and some berries. At feeders it eats mixed birdseed, sunflower seeds, niger seeds, peanuts, cracked nuts, suet, and peanut butter.

4.75 inches

Black-capped Chickadee

The Black-capped Chickadee is often seen at birdfeeders. It likes to build its nest in birdhouses. This bird is often seen with other birds such as Downy Woodpeckers, titmice, and nuthatches. Chickadees are always active and often are seen hanging upside down. The similar Carolina Chickadee is found farther south and east. It is the official bird of Maine, Massachusetts, and New Brunswick.

white cheeks

black cap

small black bill

gray back

black bib

white edges on dark wing feathers

dark-gray legs and feet

gray tail

Home Lives in forests, woods, and neighborhoods.

Voice Its *chick-a-dee-dee-dee* call is lower and slower than the Carolina Chickadee's similar call. Song is a clear, whistled *fee-bee* or *fee-bee-be*.

Food Eats insects, insect eggs, and seeds. Visits feeders for sunflower seeds, niger seeds, peanuts, cracked nuts, suet, and peanut butter.

5.5 inches

Baeolophus bicol

Tufted Titmouse

The Tufted Titmouse sings the familiar *peter, peter, peter* of early spring. Like other titmice, it will come toward you if you make squeaking or "pishing" sounds. It has even been known to eat out of a person's hand. This bird often visits feeders for sunflower seeds and peanuts. It holds the seed with its feet and hammers the shell with its bill to crack open the seed. It sometimes hangs upside down while searching for food.

dark-gray crest

gray back, wings, and tail

black bill

reddish brown sides

whitish gray breast and belly

dark-gray feet and legs

🐦 **Home** Likes damp woods, parks, and neighborhoods.

🎵 **Voice** Bold, high-pitched, whistled *peter, peter, peter* or *peto, peto, peto*. Males sing more than females. Calls vary from high, squeaky notes to low, scolding notes.

🦜 **Food** Eats seeds and insects. Visits feeders for sunflower seeds, peanuts, cracked nuts, and suet.

6.5 inches

Red-breasted Nuthatch

To protect its young from other animals, a nuthatch smears sticky sap around the entrance to its nest. The nuthatch digs a hole in a tree for its nest, or uses an old woodpecker hole. These birds often walk down a tree trunk head first. To break open the shell of a seed, a nuthatch wedges it into a crack in the bark, then hammers with its bill.

blue-gray back, wings, and tail

black cap and back of neck

white eyebrow

black eye line

white cheeks

Male

reddish brown breast and belly

lighter cream-colored breast

Female

Home Lives in woods and forests. Will use birdhouses.

Voice Its high-pitched call of *ank, ink,* or *enk* sounds like a tiny tin horn, often repeated in a rapid series.

Food Eats seeds, especially seeds from pine trees. Will eat some insects, such as moths, beetles, wasps, and caterpillars. Will come to feeders for suet, chopped nuts, and sunflower seeds.

4.5 inches

Sitta carolinens

White-breasted Nuthatch

This is the largest nuthatch in North America. Nuthatches often creep down a tree trunk head first. They circle around and beneath branches, looking for insects under the bark.

black cap and nape

long black bill

blue-gray back

white face and breast

white patches in blue-black tail

white belly

orange-brown lower belly

black feet and legs

After the White-breasted Nuthatch visits a bird feeder, it may hide seeds in a crack or crevice to save them for later meals.

🏠 **Home** Lives in woods and forests. Nests in holes in trees. Will nest in birdhouses.

🎵 **Voice** Sings *wee-wee-wee-wee-wee-wee-wee*, getting higher with each note. Its call is a hoarse *yank-yank-yank*.

🐦 **Food** Eats acorns, hickory nuts, beechnuts, and corn. Also eats moths, caterpillars, ants, flies, grasshoppers, and wood borers. Visits feeders for sunflower seeds, mixed seeds, and suet.

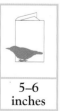

5–6 inches

Brown Creeper

The Brown Creeper roosts
hanging onto the trunk
of a tree or the side
of a house with its
sharp claws. Like
a woodpecker, it
has stiff feathers
in its tail
which it uses
to brace itself.
Watch how the
Brown Creeper
goes up a tree
searching for insects
to eat. Looking
almost like a mouse, it
circles around the trunk
as if going up a spiral
staircase to the branches.

long, thin,
curved bill

white line
over eye

white breast
and belly

sharp
claws

brown back
with buff
streaks

long reddish
brown tail with
stiff feathers

🏠 **Home** Lives in woods, forests, and wooded suburbs.

🎵 **Voice** Makes a musical *see-see-tit-see*. Its call
is a soft, thin *seee*.

🌙 **Food** Eats insects such as aphids, beetles,
caterpillars, and spiders. Some visit feeders for
peanut butter, suet, and chopped peanuts.

**5.25
inches**

Carolina Wren

The state bird of South Carolina is the largest wren in the East. The Carolina Wren holds its tail upward like most other wrens. The male sings any time of day, any day of the year. The female often answers with a quick growl of *t-shihrrr*. This wren is very active. It looks in every crack for insects.

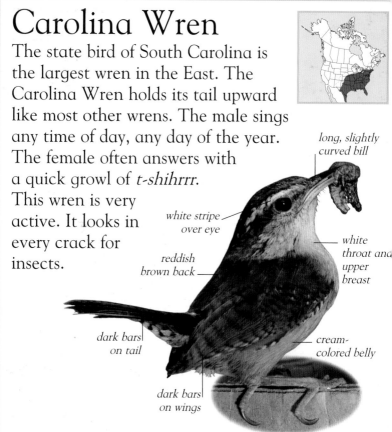

long, slightly curved bill

white stripe over eye

white throat and upper breast

reddish brown back

dark bars on tail

cream-colored belly

dark bars on wings

🏠 **Home** Lives in yards and woods. Likes brush near water.

🎵 **Voice** Song is a bold, clear *teakettle tea-kettle teakettle* or *cherry, cherry, cherry*. Males can sing 25 to 40 songs, which nearby males will copy.

🌙 **Food** Eats mostly insects but also spiders, lizards, berries, and seeds. Visits feeders for suet, sunflower seeds, nuts, peanut butter, and fruits.

5.5 inches

House Wren

This plain bird may be small, but it is
bold. The House Wren will invade
the nests of other birds and break
their eggs or kill baby birds. The male builds
several nests each spring in almost any crack
or container.

narrow,
pale eye
ring

grayish brown
back

thin black
bars on tail
and wings

thin, slightly
curved bill

pale-gray breast
and belly

thin, dark bars
on sides and
lower belly

The female
House Wren
then chooses
which nest she wants
to use and lays her eggs there. Like most wrens, the
House Wren hops about with its tail held up.

Home Lives in woods and brushy areas, on farms, in
parks, and in neighborhoods. Will nest in birdhouses.

Voice Sings a beautiful, trilling, flutelike song. Repeats
this gurgling melody after a short pause. Its call is a
rough, sharp *cheh-cheh* or a sharp chatter.

Food Eats mostly insects, such as ants,
grasshoppers, bees, and caterpillars. Also eats
spiders, millipedes, and snails.

4.75
inches

Ruby-crowned Kinglet

The small red patch on the male Ruby-crowned Kinglet's head is usually hidden. When he gets excited, he raises the feathers on his head, and the red flashes. A similar bird called the Golden-crowned Kinglet has a yellow patch with a black border on its head.

no red patch on top of head

white eye ring

two white bars on wings

Female

olive-green back

small red patch on top of head, often hidden

short black bill

white eye ring

white or creamy olive breast and belly

Male

🌲 **Home** Lives in forests. Also seen in wooded yards.

🎵 **Voice** Sings a series of high-pitched *tsee, tsee* notes, followed by several *tew* notes, then a three-note call of *liberty-liberty-liberty*. It is very loud for such a small bird. Also says *je-ditt* and *cack-cack*.

🐦 **Food** Searches for insects in trees. Also eats berries and seeds.

4.25 inches

Blue-gray Gnatcatcher

Look for the Blue-gray Gnatcatcher near the tips of branches in tall trees.

This bird is small and slender, with a long, thin bill and blue-gray feathers. Like other gnatcatchers, it has a habit of pumping its tail up and down or wagging it from side to side. It will sometimes fly out from a perch to catch flying insects.

long black tail with white outer feathers

blue-gray head and back

black line over eye in breeding plumage

white eye ring

Male

white breast and belly

no black line above eye

lighter blue-gray back and head

Female

🏠 **Home** In the East, lives in moist woods. In the West, likes thick bushes or open, dry woods.

🎵 **Voice** Sings a low-pitched, trilling *zee-you, zee-you.* Its call, *pwee?* or *speee?,* which sounds like a question, is heard more often.

🐦 **Food** Eats insects and their eggs and larvae.

4 inches

Sialia sia

Eastern Bluebird

The Eastern Bluebird likes to nest in a hole facing an open area, so farms and golf courses are good places for bluebird houses. The number of bluebirds had been decreasing because there are fewer large old trees in which they can nest. Now people build boxes for their nests, and the number of bluebirds is rising. This is the state bird of Missouri and New York.

blue head

bright-blue back and wings

reddish brown chin and throat

reddish brown breast and sides

Male

Juvenile

gray head and upper back

blue wings, lower back, and tail

reddish brown breast and sides

white belly

Female

🏠 **Home** Lives in open woods, on farms, and in orchards.

🎵 **Voice** Sings a musical *chur chur-lee chur-lee.* Males call *true-a-ly, true-a-ly.*

🪶 **Food** Eats mostly insects caught in flight or on the ground. Visits feeders for suet, mealworms, and peanut butter mixed with cornmeal.

7–8 inches

Swainson's Thrush

This thrush's repeated call of *whit* sounds like a dripping faucet. It got its name from William Swainson, a 19th-century British man who studied birds. You can tell the Swainson's Thrush from other similar-looking thrushes by its cream-colored cheeks and eye ring.

cream-colored eye ring

black bill

creamy olive-brown head

cream-colored cheeks and throat

creamy olive-brown back, wings, and tail

blurry, dark spots on creamy breast

pale-gray belly

pink legs and feet

🏠 **Home** Lives in moist forests and thickets. Likes willows and maples beside streams. Spends winter from Mexico to South America.

🎵 **Voice** Sings a rising series of thin, musical, whistling notes, which it repeats after pausing.

🐛 **Food** Eats insects, snails, and earthworms. In winter and migration it eats more fruits and berries.

7 inches

Hylocichla mustelin

Wood Thrush

You may not see this bird perched up high, but you will hear its flutelike song. To see it, look close to the ground, where it will be eating. Thrushes pick insects and berries from low branches or fallen leaves.

reddish brown crown and nape

white ring around large, dark eye

reddish brown back

brown tail

white face with black streaks

large, dark spots on breast, belly, and sides

When a Wood Thrush gets excited, it raises the feathers on its head. This is the official bird of the District of Columbia.

pinkish legs and feet

🏠 **Home** Lives in woods, forests, parks, and yards.

🎵 **Voice** A peaceful, flutelike series of three phrases, with the middle note lower than the first and the last note highest and trilled, *ee-o-lee, ee-o-lay.* Calls out with a rough-sounding *quirt* or fast *pit, pit, pit.*

🌑 **Food** Eats insects, spiders, fruits, and berries. Visits platform feeders for birdseed, suet, or fruits.

8 inches

American Robin

The return of the robin is thought to be a sign that spring has come. But the robin stays year-round in many areas. You may see a robin turn its head to the side while it hops on the ground. People once thought the bird was listening for worms. The real reason that the robin tips its head is so it can better see the worms. This is the state bird of Connecticut, Michigan, and Wisconsin.

blackish head

yellow bill

broken eye ring

dark brownish gray back

brick-red breast

Juvenile

Male

white lower belly

brownish gray head

brownish orange breast

Female

🏠 **Home** Lives all over in woods, fields, meadows, parks, towns, and neighborhoods. Uses nesting shelves and birdbaths.

🎵 **Voice** Sings a gurgling, slow, sing-song *cheerily cheer-up cheerio*, often repeated. Rapidly calls *tut-tut-tut* or *hip-hip-hip*.

🪱 **Food** Eats worms, insects, fruits, and berries. Visits flat feeders for chopped nuts, suet, or fruits.

10 inches

Dumetella carolinens

Gray Catbird

A catbird makes catlike mewing sounds, which is how the bird got its name. A catbird usually stays low in thick brush, often holding its tail up and flicking it from side to side. Catbirds, along with mockingbirds, belong to the mimic thrush family. A mimic thrush mimics, or copies, the sounds of other birds, frogs, and even machines.

black cap

slate-gray back

black tail

dark bill

reddish brown under tail

paler gray breast and belly

slate-gray wings

dark legs

Home Lives in thickets and brush, as well as in neighborhoods and gardens.

Voice Sings a mixture of sweet to harsh phrases. Mimics other birds. Call is a quiet *mew*. Also a harsh *quit* or *chack*.

Food Eats many kinds of insects, spiders, millipedes, centipedes, and berries. Visits feeders for cereals, raisins, and other fruits.

8–9 inches

Northern Mockingbird

The mockingbird sings its best on warm, moonlit nights. It imitates the songs of other birds, as well as other sounds. It has even been heard barking like a dog. A mockingbird protects its territory and will swoop at people, cats, and dogs – even its own reflection in a window. The mockingbird has a habit of flicking its tail. This is the state bird of Arkansas, Florida, Mississippi, Tennessee, and Texas.

thin, dark line through eye

gray head and back

long, dark tail with white outer feathers

large white patches on dark wings

two white wing bars

Juvenile

Home Lives in scrubby woodlands, desert brush, canyons, farms, parks, and neighborhoods.

Voice Sings a variety of its own songs and imitates other birds. Repeats phrases three to five times. Has a loud, harsh *check* call.

Food Eats insects, spiders, crayfish, lizards, berries, and fruits. Visits feeders for peanut butter, chopped nuts, suet, bread, and raisins.

10 inches

Brown Thrasher

Look for this bird on the ground. Thrashers are named for their habit of thrashing about, tossing up leaves with their bills while looking for insects. The Brown Thrasher is sometimes confused with the Wood Thrush but has yellow eyes and a much longer tail. The Brown Thrasher, Georgia's state bird, is the only thrasher found in the East.

yellow eye

curved bill

reddish brown head and back

white breast with dark-brown streaks

two white wing bars

white belly with dark-brown streaks

long reddish brown tail

🏠 **Home** Likes thickets, the edges of woods, and brush along fences.

🎵 **Voice** Male sings phrases that sound like *hello, hello, yes, yes, who is this? who is this? I should say, I should say.* More than a thousand different songs have been recorded. Has a sharp call of *smack* or *churr.*

🐦 **Food** Eats insects, berries, acorns, and grains.

11–12 inches

European Starling

About 60 European Starlings were brought over from Europe and released in New York in 1890. This was part of a project to bring to America every bird mentioned in William Shakespeare's plays. Since then, starlings have spread to all of the United States and much of Canada. These birds gather in large flocks that are noisy and messy. They damage crops and compete for nesting sites with other birds that nest in holes.

black body with purple-green gloss (speckled white in fall and winter)

short tail

yellow bill with blue base (female has pink bill)

pinkish legs

Juvenile

🚶 **Home** Lives in cities, neighborhoods, orchards, woods, and on farms and ranches. Nests in birdhouses.

🎵 **Voice** Sings trilling melodies, clear whistles, clatters, and twitters. Imitates other birds and machine sounds. Also makes a flutelike *pheeEW*.

🐦 **Food** Hunts on the ground for insects. Also eats worms, fruits, berries, seeds, and grain.

8.5 inches

Cedar Waxwing

The Cedar Waxwing tends to travel in flocks. You often find 50 or more of them feeding in trees or bushes with berries. Sometimes you see the waxwing on the ground, picking up fallen berries or drinking from a puddle. This bird is called a waxwing because there are hard, waxlike red tips on some of its wing feathers. Waxwings have been seen passing a berry or flower down a row of birds, from one to the next, until one of the birds eats it.

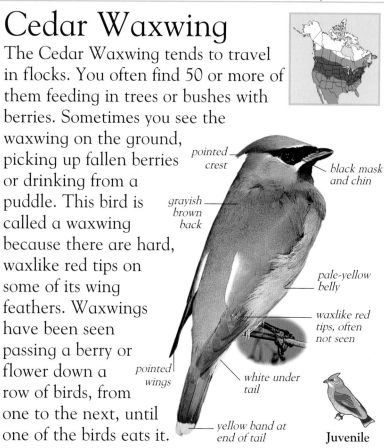

pointed crest

black mask and chin

grayish brown back

pale-yellow belly

waxlike red tips, often not seen

pointed wings

white under tail

yellow band at end of tail

Juvenile

🌲 **Home** Lives in neighborhoods, orchards, woods, and city parks.

🎵 **Voice** Call is a thin, high *zeeee* or *zeeeet*.

🐦 **Food** Eats fruits, berries, flower petals, maple tree sap, and insects. It is attracted to yards with mountain ash and cedar trees.

7 inches

Northern Parula

The Northern Parula likes to use Spanish moss in the South, or lichens in the North, when it builds its nest. Look for this bird in trees where these plants grow, and you will see it moving around like an acrobat. It may be searching for nesting materials or looking on tree trunks, leaves, and branches for insects and caterpillars. This is one of the smallest warblers.

broken white eye ring

blue-gray head and back

yellow throat and breast

two white wing bars

male has reddish and gray bands on breast

white belly

Home Nests in wet forests and swamps and along lakes and ponds. Winters in Mexico and the West Indies.

Voice Its buzzy *zeeeeeeee-yip* song rises, then drops at the end like a cup filling with song and spilling over the top. Has a sharp call of *chip*.

Food Eats mostly insects, including small beetles, ants, bees, scale insects, and caterpillars. Also eats spiders.

4 inches

Dendroica petechia

Yellow Warbler

The Yellow Warbler looks all-yellow when seen from a distance. Up close, though, you can see the dark colors in the wings, red streaks on the breast, and the yellow dots on its tail. This bird has the widest breeding range of all the warblers in North America. In summer it can be found from Virginia to California and from Canada to Mexico.

yellow-olive back, wings, and tail

bright-yellow head

dark eyes

yellow edges on dark flight feathers

yellow breast and belly with red streaks

Male

yellow-green back, wings, and tail

fewer faint red streaks on breast

Female

Home Likes thickets, especially willows and alders, along creeks, streams, and swampy areas. Also in neighborhoods.

Voice Sings a varied, swift, warbling *sweet-sweet, I'm so sweet* or *tseet-tseet-tseet-titi-deet*.

Food Searches trees and bushes for insects and insect larvae, including beetles, weevils, and caterpillars. Will also eat some fruits.

5 inches

Yellow-rumped Warbler

This warbler remains farther north in winter than other warblers. Even when the male's feathers change color in the winter, this bird can be identified by the patch of yellow on the rump. You might see this bird in big flocks. Eastern birds have white throats, and western birds have yellow throats.

streaked back

Female

streaked breast and belly

yellow patch on crown

two white wing bars

Male

yellow rump

streaks on sides

black face patch

black on breast

yellow side patches

Fall adult

Winter adult

🏠 **Home** Lives in woods, forests, and wooded yards.

🎵 **Voice** Various slow warbles that slow down in the middle, then speed up. Each song ends with either rising or falling notes. Some have a musical *trill*. Call is a loud *check, chup,* or *chip.*

🐦 **Food** Eats mostly insects, but will eat berries and seeds. Visits feeders for sunflower seeds, suet, or peanut butter.

5.5 inches

Mniotilta var

Black-and-white Warbler

The Black-and-white Warbler creeps along tree trunks and over and around branches, looking for insects in the bark. Other warblers flit from branch to branch.

black-and-white stripes on head and body

white stripe over and under each eye

black cheek

short, square tail

white belly

Although this bird feeds in trees, it builds its nest on or near the ground. Look for this warbler by itself, in pairs, or in flocks of other birds.

Home Lives in woods and forests.

Voice Repeats a thin, high series of six to ten *wee-sea, wee-sea* notes, like the sound of a squeaky wheel. Sometimes adds a trill at the end. Call is a rough *chip* or *tink* and a *seap*.

Food Eats caterpillars and insects, such as moths, ants, and beetles. Also eats spiders.

5 inches

American Redstart

In Cuba and other Latin American countries, this warbler is called *Candelita* or "little torch." It flits about in the tops of trees like a spark of fire. No other warbler has a similar pattern of orange and black on the wings and tail. This bird has a habit of drooping its wings and fanning its tail before leaping out to catch insects in the air.

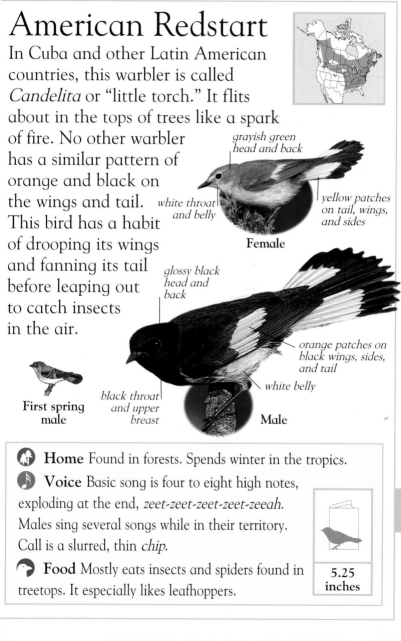

grayish green head and back

yellow patches on tail, wings, and sides

white throat and belly

Female

glossy black head and back

orange patches on black wings, sides, and tail

white belly

black throat and upper breast

Male

First spring male

Home Found in forests. Spends winter in the tropics.

Voice Basic song is four to eight high notes, exploding at the end, *zeet-zeet-zeet-zeet-zeeah*. Males sing several songs while in their territory. Call is a slurred, thin *chip*.

Food Mostly eats insects and spiders found in treetops. It especially likes leafhoppers.

5.25 inches

Ovenbird

Unlike most other warblers, which feed in the trees, this bird searches for insects among fallen leaves on the forest floor. Its name comes from the oven-shaped nest the female builds. The nest has a roof and a side entrance.

brownish orange stripe on head, edged with black

white eye ring

greenish brown back and wings

It is called the "teacher bird" because of its song. Chances are, you will hear this bird before you see it.

white breast and belly with heavy dark streaks

pinkish legs

🌲 **Home** Lives in older, dry forests that are open below the tree branches.

🎵 **Voice** Repeats a loud *TEAcher-TEAcher-TEAcher*, getting higher and stronger. Some sing *teach-teach-teach-teACH!* From a distance, it sounds like two stones being tapped together harder and harder. Call is a loud, sharp *tsick*.

🐦 **Food** Eats mostly insects such as ants.

6 inches

Common Yellowthroat

Look for the Yellowthroat close to the ground in wild, tangled areas, such as briers, cattails, or overgrown creek banks. The female looks plain and can be difficult to tell from some other female and juvenile warblers. The Yellowthroat has a habit of flicking its tail and drooping, then flicking, its wings. This is one of the most widespread warblers in North America.

black mask with whitish border on top

greenish gray head, back, and wings

Male

bright-yellow throat and breast

white belly

Juvenile

pale eye ring

pale-yellow breast and throat

Female

Home Lives in marshes, meadows, and other moist areas with thickets.

Voice Its song sounds like *wichity wichity wich*, and it can vary. Sharp, raspy calls of *chuck* or *djip*. Sometimes gives a flat *pit*.

Food Eats insects and spiders.

5 inches

Yellow-breasted Chat

The chat is the largest warbler in North America. Unlike other warblers, it often sings at night, as well as during the day. Other warblers also have a thinner bill. The chat usually stays undercover in thick brush.

brownish green head

long brownish green tail

white eye ring goes to bill

white belly

thick bill

brownish green back and wings

black spot in front of eye

bright-yellow throat and breast

When it flies from one bush to another, its legs dangle down and its wings flop, making it look awkward.

Home Lives in thickets on hillsides or near streams.

Voice Mixture of whistles, catlike sounds, clucking, and screeching that can sound musical or harsh. Calls are a harsh *heow* or a nasal *hair*.

Food Eats mostly insects, including ants, bees, beetles, and caterpillars. Also likes berries such as strawberries, blackberries, and raspberries.

7 inches

Scarlet Tanager

In the summer, no other bird looks like the male Scarlet Tanager, with his bright-red body and black wings and tail. By fall, this bird has molted. Then he looks more like the female with a dull-green and yellow body, although the wings and tail are black.

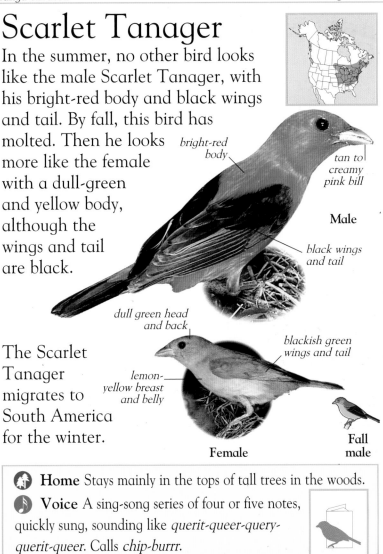

bright-red body

tan to creamy pink bill

Male

black wings and tail

dull green head and back

blackish green wings and tail

lemon-yellow breast and belly

The Scarlet Tanager migrates to South America for the winter.

Female

Fall male

🌲 **Home** Stays mainly in the tops of tall trees in the woods.

🎵 **Voice** A sing-song series of four or five notes, quickly sung, sounding like *querit-queer-query-querit-queer*. Calls *chip-burrr*.

🐛 **Food** Hunts insects, caterpillars, and spiders. Often visits fruit and berry trees or bushes.

7 inches

Eastern Towhee

Some people confuse towhees with American Robins. However, the Eastern Towhee has a black throat and upper breast, with reddish brown only on the sides. The robin has a solid reddish brown breast. Towhees are often seen near bushes, scratching for insects in fallen leaves, pulling both legs back at the same time. Towhees are related to sparrows.

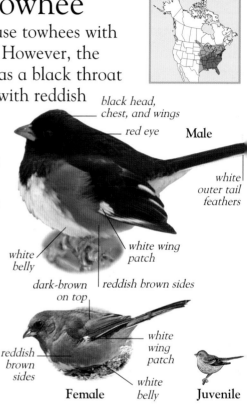

black head, chest, and wings

red eye **Male**

white outer tail feathers

white wing patch

white belly

reddish brown sides

dark-brown on top

white wing patch

reddish brown sides

white belly

Female

Juvenile

🏠 **Home** Lives at forest edges and in brushy woods, thickets, neighborhoods, and parks.

🎵 **Voice** Many variations of a clear, whistled *drink-your-teeeaaa*, with "tea" trilled. Has calls of *toe-WHEEE* and *che-winck* or *che-wanck*.

🌙 **Food** Scratches for insects in fallen leaves under shrubs. Also eats seeds and fruits.

7–7.5 inches

Chipping Sparrow

Named for its song – a series of chipping sounds – this bird likes to sing from a high perch. Sometimes it sings at night as well as during the day. The Chipping Sparrow is often found near people. Nests have been found in yards and cemeteries and on golf courses.

heavy white line over eye

bright reddish brown cap

thin black line through eye

gray cheek and neck

clear gray breast and belly

two white wing bars

long, notched tail

streaked brown-and-black back and wings

This bird often joins a flock with other sparrows in the winter.

Juvenile

Winter adult

🐦 **Home** Lives at the edges of woods and in brushy pastures, parks, orchards, and neighborhoods. Likes pine trees.

🎵 **Voice** Repeats a series of trilled chip notes, *chip-chip-chip-chip-chip-chip-chip*, all in the same pitch. Has a call of *seek*.

🌰 **Food** Eats mainly seeds, especially grass seeds. Also eats insects. Will peck at salt blocks. Visits feeders for bread crumbs and seeds.

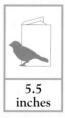

5.5 inches

Savannah Sparrow

You might think this bird was named for the grassy habitat where it lives. However, it was named for the city of Savannah, Georgia, where Alexander Wilson discovered it in 1811. There are at least 17 races of Savannah Sparrows. So, this bird can look slightly different in various areas. Look for this sparrow on the ground, where it spends most of its time looking for food.

yellow or white eyebrow stripe

heavy streaks on breast and sides

pinkish feet and legs

short, notched tail

🌲 **Home** Likes open areas such as savannah, hay fields, salt marshes, wet meadows, and tundra.

🎵 **Voice** Song begins with two or three *chip* notes, followed by two buzzy, insectlike trills, *tip-tip-seeeee-saaaay*. Its call is *seep*.

🐦 **Food** Scratches on the ground for food, including seeds, grasses, insects, spiders, and sometimes snails.

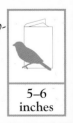

5–6 inches

Song Sparrow

The Song Sparrow sometimes sings for as long as two hours at a time. That is how this bird got its name. This sparrow varies in size and color from very light to very dark races. One thing they all have in common is that they pump their tails when they fly.

broad grayish eyebrow

streaked brownish gray body

white throat

streaked breast

long, rounded tail

pinkish feet and legs

Dark race

The Song Sparrow is usually found alone or in pairs. In winter, it may flock with other birds.

Home Might be found anywhere, but seems to especially like brushy areas near water.

Voice There are differences among birds, but the song is one of the best ways to identify this sparrow. It whistles two or three clear notes, followed by a *trill*. Has calls of *chimp* or *what*, and a high, thin *ssst*.

Food Eats seeds, insects, berries, and fruits. Visits feeders for birdseed.

6–7.5 inches

White-throated Sparrow

This is one of the easiest eastern sparrows to identify. Look for its broad yellow eyebrows, bold stripes on the head, dark bill, and white throat outlined with black. You will see this bird in your yard, scratching in leaves on the ground, where it looks for fallen seeds and berries. A similar bird, the White-crowned Sparrow, can be seen in winter in the Southeast. It does not have yellow eyebrows.

yellow eyebrow

dark stripes on head

streaked reddish brown back

white throat has black outline

two white wing bars

grayish belly and breast can be streaked

Juvenile

🏠 **Home** Likes brushy areas in woods, pastures, marshes, and yards.

🎵 **Voice** A thin whistle that starts with two single notes, followed by three triple notes: *poor-sam-peabody, peabody-peabody* or *pure-sweet-Canada-Canada-Canada.* Calls include *pink* and *tseep.*

🌰 **Food** Eats mostly weed seeds. Also eats berries, fruits, tree buds, and insects.

6–8 inches

Dark-eyed Junco

Small flocks of juncos are usually seen eating and hopping on the ground, looking for food. Sometimes you find them in low bushes. Notice their white outer tail feathers when they fly. Juncos build their nests on the ground in hidden places, such as under fallen logs. There are five races of the Dark-eyed Junco. Juncos are in the sparrow family.

brownish gray head and back

Slate-colored female

Pink-sided male

dark-gray head and back

White-winged male

Gray-headed male

white outer tail feathers

Slate-colored male

Oregon male

🌲 **Home** Lives in woods, brushy areas, fields, and yards.

🎵 **Voice** Musical trill, varied in pitch and speed, from *chip* notes to bell-like sounds. Call is a rough *dit* with a smacking sound. Twitters while in flight.

🐦 **Food** Eats seeds, nuts, grains, and some insects. Visits flat feeders for seeds and nuts.

6 inches

Cardinalis cardinal

Northern Cardinal

You can see why this bird is nicknamed the Redbird. The Northern Cardinal is the state bird of Illinois, Indiana, Kentucky, North Carolina, Ohio, Virginia, and West Virginia. Cardinals do not walk – they hop. These birds do not migrate to warmer places for the winter. You can enjoy them at your feeder year-round.

large crest

black mask

cone-shaped reddish bill

red body

Male

red tip on crest

brownish back

light-brown breast

Female

Juvenile

Home Lives in thickets, parks, gardens, and yards.

Voice Sings more than 25 songs, including *whoit cheer, whoit cheer, cheer-cheer-cheer, cheer, whoit-whoit-whoit-whoit, wheat-wheat-wheat-wheat,* and *bir-dy, bir-dy, bir-dy, bir-dy.* Call is a metallic *chip* or *pik.*

Food Eats insects, seeds, fruits, and grains. Visits feeders for sunflower seeds, cracked corn, and birdseed.

7.5–9 inches

Rose-breasted Grosbeak

With his rose-red bib, the male Rose-breasted Grosbeak is hard to mistake. When he flies, you can see red under his wings, too. Like other grosbeaks, this bird uses its powerful bill to crack open seeds. Grosbeaks hunt for food both in trees and on the ground.

black head and back

white wing patches

Male

heavy, pale bill

red triangle on breast

white belly

Juvenile male

white eyebrow

streaked brown back

darker bill

Female

streaked breast

First spring male

🏠 **Home** Lives along streams and in woods, pastures, and parks. Migrates as far as South America for winter.

🎵 **Voice** Rich, warbled, musical phrases with *eek* call notes in between.

🐛 **Food** Eats mostly insects in summer. The rest of the year it eats seeds and fruits. Visits feeders for sunflower seeds.

7–8.5 inches

Blue Grosbeak

This bird likes to sing from the top of a post, wire, or tree. The Blue Grosbeak has a habit of flicking and spreading its tail. From a distance this bird may look black. Up close you can see its deep-blue feathers. Look for its silvery-white bill. Grosbeaks search for food in trees and bushes and on the ground. In the fall, Blue Grosbeaks form large flocks that feed in weedy fields.

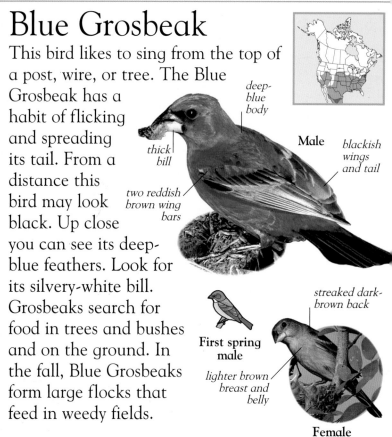

deep-blue body

Male

blackish wings and tail

thick bill

two reddish brown wing bars

First spring male

streaked dark-brown back

lighter brown breast and belly

Female

🏠 **Home** Found in hedgerows, along wooded streams, and in brushy fields.

🎵 **Voice** Series of deep, rich, slightly scratchy warbles that rise and fall in pitch. Its call is an explosive, metallic *pink*.

🐦 **Food** Eats insects, seeds, and fruits. Visits feeders for sunflower seeds and grains.

6–7.5 inches

Indigo Bunting

In the sunlight, the male Indigo Bunting looks bright blue. In the shade, you might think he is black. Look for this bird in hedgerows in the country. The male often perches in treetops to sing. During nesting season, he will chase other birds out of his territory. The Indigo Bunting hunts for food in trees, in bushes, and on the ground.

thick bill

bright-blue body

Male

blue edges on blackish wing and tail feathers

brown head and back

Juvenile

whitish throat, breast, and belly

blue edges on dark-brown wing and tail feathers

Female

Winter male

🏠 **Home** Likes brushy areas in fields and woods.

🎵 **Voice** Series of varied phrases, usually in pairs, _sweet-sweet, sweeter-sweeter, here-here,_ often with a trilled ending. Calls _spit_ or _plik._

🪶 **Food** Eats insects, seeds, grains, and berries. Visits feeders for small seeds and grains.

5–6 inches

Painted Bunting

The male Painted Bunting looks like it flew into an artist's paint set. No other North American bird has so many bright colors. Unlike many species, the male keeps his bright colors all year. This bird looks for food on the ground and in bushes and low trees. It is shy, so you will not see it often. In winter it may visit southern feeders.

deep blue-purple head and neck

bright lime-green back

red eye ring

Male

red breast and belly

dark-gray feathers on tail and wings have red edges

green head and back

Juvenile

gray-green wings and tail

yellow-green breast and belly

Female

🐦 **Home** Lives in thickets, hedgerows, and briar patches.

🎵 **Voice** High-pitched, musical warble, *pew-eata, pew-eata, I eaty you too.* Has a two-note chip or a "wet" *plik* call.

🌙 **Food** Eats mainly grass seeds. Also eats other seeds and insects. Visits feeders for birdseed and sunflower seeds. Enjoys birdbaths.

5–5.5 inches

House Finch

The House Finch once lived only in the West. In the 1940s, some of these birds were taken to New York as pet birds in cages. Some escaped or were set free. Now they live all over North America. The House Finch often nests in potted plants. In the East it nests in spruce trees found in yards. It might also nest in holes in trees or in a birdhouse.

reddish crown

streaked brown back and wings

Male

bright-red bib

two thin white wing bars

streaked brown sides

streaked brown head, back, and wings

two whitish wing bars

brown streaks on cream-colored breast and belly

Female

🐦 **Home** Lives in many places, including cities, desert brush, orchards, and yards.

🎵 **Voice** Near the nest it makes a *witchew, witchew, witchew*.

🪶 **Food** Eats weed seeds, fruits, blossoms, buds, and insects. Visits feeders for thistle, sunflower, millet, and other seeds.

6 inches

Red Crossbill

It is easy to see how this finch got its name. The tips of its bill cross instead of coming straight together. This bill works well to pry seeds from pine cones. Young birds have straight bills when they hatch. Their bills grow crooked soon after they leave the nest. The Red Crossbill is unusual because it may nest at any time of year, depending on the pine cone crop.

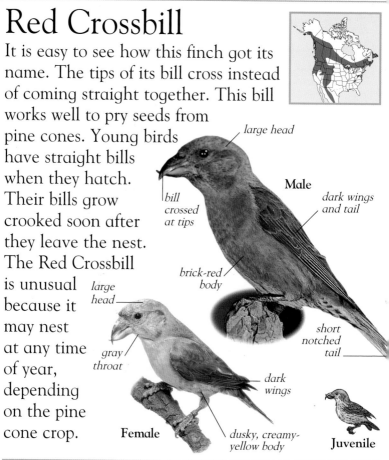

large head

Male

bill crossed at tips

dark wings and tail

brick-red body

short notched tail

large head

gray throat

dark wings

Female

dusky, creamy-yellow body

Juvenile

Home Lives in pine forests and visits pine trees in yards.

Voice Series of two-note phrases followed by a trilled warble that sounds like *jitt-jitt-jitt-jitt, jiiaa-jiiaa-jiiaaaaa*. Songs can vary.

Food Eats mostly pine seeds but also insects. Visits feeders for sunflower seeds.

5.5–6.5 inches

Pine Siskin

The Pine Siskin looks a little like a
sparrow with yellow wing bars. Siskins
search for seeds on pine, hemlock,
spruce, alder, and birch trees. The
Pine Siskin is a very active bird
that gathers in large flocks in
the winter and is often found
in flocks with goldfinches
and other birds. Siskins
can wander far from
their normal range
in winter.

streaked brown
head, back,
and wings

thin
bill

white breast
and belly
with brown
streaks

yellow edges on
wing flight
feathers

yellow at
base of tail

notched,
dark tail

🐦 **Home** Lives in evergreen forests and woods.

🎵 **Voice** Husky, twittering warble, rising and falling in
pitch with an occasional *ZZZzzzzzrree!* that sounds
like a tiny chainsaw. Call is rising *tee-e.* Flight note
is hoarse *chee* that lowers as the bird goes.

🌙 **Food** Eats seeds, flower buds, and insects.
Visits feeders for mixed seed, sunflower seed, and
thistle seeds. Enjoys birdbaths.

4.5–5
inches

Carduelis tris

American Goldfinch

In the breeding season, the male is bright-yellow and black. In the winter, he turns dusty brown with black wings and tail and looks more like the female. Goldfinches' favorite food is thistle seeds. Sometimes they visit flower gardens to eat the seeds of zinnias and other flowers. Goldfinches travel in flocks. This is the state bird of Iowa, New Jersey, and Washington.

black cap

Male

bright-yellow body

black wings with two white wing bars

black-and-white tail

greenish gray back

dull-yellow breast and belly

Female

Juvenile

Winter male   **Winter female**

Home Likes trees with seeds, weedy fields, and thickets.

Voice A jumbled series of musical warbles and trills, often with a long *baybee* note. Its flight song sounds like *per-chick-oree* or *po-tato-chips*.

Food Eats seeds, berries, and insects. Visits feeders for thistle seeds and sunflower seeds.

5 inches

House Sparrow

This bird originally lived in Europe. Some were set free in New York in the 1850s. People hoped they would eat canker worms that were hurting trees in city parks. Because the House Sparrow adapts easily to new habitats, especially near people, it quickly spread across North America. The House Sparrow builds nests in gutters and cracks in buildings and can be found in places other birds avoid.

gray crown and cheeks

reddish brown from eye to back of neck

streaked brown wings

black bill

black bib

Male

white wing bar

gray sides and belly

cream-colored eyebrow

Winter male

dark stripe behind eye

no black bib

brownish gray breast and belly

Female

🏠 **Home** Lives in cities, towns, and yards, as well as on farms and ranches. Likes to nest in birdhouses.

🎵 **Voice** Makes a twittering series of *chirps*. Its call is a plain, repeated *cheep-cheep-cheep*.

🐛 **Food** Eats insects, fruits, seeds, and grains. Visits feeders for bread, seeds, and grains.

5.5–6.5 inches

Dolichonyx oryzivoru

Bobolink

The male sings its name, *bob-o-link*, in a happy song. Many birds have lighter colored feathers on their belly and darker colored feathers on their backs. The Bobolink is different. Some people say the male Bobolink looks as if he is wearing his suit backward. These birds gather in large flocks of hundreds of Bobolinks, which sweep across fields. They are nicknamed Ricebirds because they often eat rice crops.

front of head is black

black bill

black breast, belly, and wings

back of head is creamy yellow

large white shoulder patch

white rump

Male

pointed black tail feathers

striped head

streaked back, wings, and sides

pinkish bill

Female

Winter male

🌲 **Home** Found in farmlands, meadows, and prairies.

🎵 **Voice** Lively, bubbling series of notes, starting low then bouncing up, *bob-o-link, bob-o-link, pink, pink, pank, pink.* Call is clear *pink.*

🦅 **Food** Eats weed seeds, grass seeds, rice, grains, and insects.

6–8 inches

Red-winged Blackbird

This common, widespread bird is often found in fields and marshes. In late summer and winter, the Red-winged Blackbird joins cowbirds, grackles, and starlings to form flocks of thousands of birds. They swarm down, like a noisy black cloud, and fill trees or lawns. A flock can cover a whole neighborhood block. The birds hop or run across the ground, trying to get their share of food.

sharp, pointed bill

red shoulder patch with yellow edge

Male

black body

First year male

tan stripe over eye

whitish breast and belly with streaks

streaked brown back and wings

Female

🏠 **Home** Lives in marshes, swamps, pastures, and meadows.

🎵 **Voice** Gurgling, reedy *konk-la-ree* or *gurr-ga-lee*. Calls are a low *clack*, a sharp nasal *deekk*, and a metallic *tiink*.

🍽 **Food** Eats mostly weed seeds and grains, plus insects, berries, snails, and mollusks. Visits yards for bread and birdseed.

7.5–9.5 inches

Eastern Meadowlark

Look for this bird feeding in a pasture or singing on a fence post or wire. Meadowlarks walk around on the ground, using their bills to probe for food. In the summer you will see this bird alone or in pairs. In the winter it forms small flocks. Meadowlarks build their nests on the ground. Sometimes nests are destroyed when fields are mowed. The very similar Western Meadowlark is found farther west.

black-and-white striped crown

brown back and wings streaked with black

white face

broad black V on breast

yellow breast and belly

white sides with black spots and streaks

white outer tail feathers

🌲 **Home** Found in meadows, on farms and prairies, or beside country roads.

🎵 **Voice** Sings a sad-sounding *tee-you, tee-airrr* or *spring-o'-the-year.* Its call from the ground or during flight is a high, buzzy *zzzzrrt.* Another flight call is a nasal *sweeink.*

🐦 **Food** Eats mostly insects and spiders. Also eats seeds, grains, and tender plants.

9–11 inches

Common Grackle

Grackles eat, roost, and nest in a group all year. In winter, the Common Grackle can be found in huge, noisy flocks with thousands of blackbirds, starlings, and cowbirds. When a male Common Grackle wants to impress a female, he fluffs out the feathers on his shoulders, droops his wings, and sings.

pale-yellow eyes

purple or bronze shine on back

long, sharp bill

purplish shine on head, neck, and breast

long tail

glossy black body

purple shine on head and neck

Male

dull black body

Female

Home Found in fields, parks, farms, woods, and lawns. Also lives near marshes.

Voice Squeaky *coguba-leek* sounds like a creaking rusty hinge. Call is a bold *chuk*.

Food Eats many foods, including insects, worms, minnows, crayfish, frogs, salamanders, mice, small birds and birds' eggs, seeds, grains, acorns, nuts, and fruits. Visits yards for cracked corn, seeds, and grains placed on the ground.

11–13.5 inches

Boat-tailed Grackle

This large bird is found along the coasts and across Florida, where it is never far from the water. The Boat-tailed Grackle walks along the edge of the water, looking for fish and other food.

yellow or brown eye

very long tail

Male

black body with blue shine

This long-tailed bird often perches in trees or on wires, where it sings its loud song. There are different races of this grackle. Their eyes can be brown or yellow.

lighter brown face, breast, and belly

dark-brown back, wings, and tail

Female

Home Lives in marshes or near beaches, farms, towns, and other areas close to water.

Voice Repeats a rough, loud *jeeb, jeeb, jeeb*. Makes a noisy variety of harsh whistles, chucks, rattles, and raspy clicks.

Food Eats fish, frogs, snails, insects, shrimp, small birds, small reptiles, fruits, grains, and seeds.

12–17 inches

Brown-headed Cowbird

A cowbird never raises its own young. The female lays a single egg in the nest of another bird, often tossing out the other bird's eggs. Even if some of the original eggs remain, the young cowbird often hatches first. By the time the others hatch the cowbird is older and bigger, so it usually gets more food from its foster parent than the others do. Once the cowbird leaves its foster nest, it will join a flock with other cowbirds and blackbirds.

brown head

short, thick bill

black body with faint green sheen

Male

brownish gray head and back

lighter brownish gray breast and belly

Female

Juvenile

🌲 **Home** Found in fields and pastures. Also lives in parks, woods, and yards, and along streams.

🎵 **Voice** Courtship song is a gurgling *glug-glug-glee*. A female calls with a harsh rattle. A male in flight has a high, slurred *ts-eeeu*.

🐦 **Food** Eats grains, seeds, insects, and berries.

7–8 inches

Orchard Oriole

This oriole got its name because it is sometimes seen in orchards. It spends most of its time in neighborhood trees or trees near farms. Orioles eat some fruits, but insects make up most of their diet. Orioles build some of the most unusual nests of all birds. The nest is usually a woven basket or bag that hangs from the branch of a tree.

black head, back, and wings

Male

one white wing bar

reddish brown shoulder

reddish brown breast, belly, and sides

olive-green head and back

black tail

yellowish breast and belly

First spring male

Female

🌳 **Home** Found in trees in orchards and towns, on prairies along streams, and on farms. Spends winter in the tropics.

🎵 **Voice** Sings a loud variety of whistled notes, speeding up into a jumbled ending with a slurred *wheer!*, sounding like *look here, what cheer, wee yo, what cheer, whip yo, what wheer!* Calls are a sharp but musical *chuk* and a chattering *chuh-huh-huh-huh.*

🐦 **Food** Eats insects, spiders, and fruits.

6–8 inches

Baltimore Oriole

This is the state bird of Maryland. In the breeding season these birds live alone or in pairs. Look for them in trees and bushes where they search for insects and caterpillars among the leaves. Orioles weave their nests in the shape of a bag or basket that hangs from a tree branch.

black head, back, and wings

orange breast and belly

orange shoulder patch

white wing bar

Male

orange-and-black tail

black on head and throat

olive-brown back, wings, and tail

dull-yellow breast

Female

two white wing bars

First fall male

First fall female

🐦 **Home** Lives in woods, neighborhoods, orchards, and trees near streams. Migrates to the tropics for the winter.

🎵 **Voice** Sings two-note, whistled, musical phrases, some with long pauses, *hue-lee, hue-lee, hue-lee*. Calls *hue-le*e. Also cries *caw-caw-caw-caw-caw*.

🌓 **Food** Eats mostly insects and caterpillars but also fruits and berries. Visits feeders for oranges, peanut butter, suet, and sugar water.

7–8 inches

Glossary

Adapt - to change to fit into a new place.

Aphid - a small insect that sucks the juices from plants.

Binoculars - a telescope you hold up to both eyes to make objects appear closer and larger.

Bird of prey - a bird that hunts other animals for food; an eagle or owl, for example.

Breed - *verb,* to produce baby birds.

Breeding grounds - where a bird nests and raises its young.

Breeding plumage - a bird's feathers during spring and summer, at which time the bird is mating and raising young birds. In many species, the breeding plumage has brighter colors than the plumage of fall and winter.

Burrow - *noun,* a tunnel or hole in the ground.

Camouflage - feathers, clothing, or fur with a color or pattern that blends into a background.

Canyon - a narrow valley with steep sides.

Chaparral - a thick area of bushes or shrubs.

Colony - a group of birds that live close together.

Conservation - the protection and improvement of natural resources to protect plants and animals for the benefit of everyone.

Contour feathers - the feathers found on the bird's body.

Courtship - when a male tries to attract a female.

Covey - a small flock of birds; quail, for example.

Crest - a pointed tuft of feathers on a bird's head.

Crop - 1. A special sack in the throat of birds, used mainly to store food. 2. Plants grown on farms.

Crown - the top of the head.

Crustaceans - a class of small animals that have an outer shell and usually live in the water; includes shrimp and crabs.

Dabble - the feeding method of some ducks; from the surface of the water, the duck tips up its rump and sticks its head into the water to reach plants and seeds.

Dabbling duck - a duck that feeds from the surface of the water by tipping up its rump and putting its head in the water.

Down - small, fluffy feathers that grow underneath the contour feathers of a bird.

Endangered - a species that is in serious trouble and could face extinction in the near future. It is against the law to own or hurt an endangered species.

Family - a group of bird species with many things in common.

Fledgling - a young bird that is learning to fly.

Flight feathers - long feathers on the wings and tail that help a bird fly.

Flock - *noun*, a group of birds traveling or feeding together. *Verb*, to gather in a group with other birds.

Forage - to look for food.

Habit - a tendency to act in a certain way; a repeated activity.

Habitat - the natural home of a bird or other animal, or the characteristics of an area, including its climate and plants.

Hibernate - to spend the winter in a deep sleep.

Hover - a special type of flight that allows a bird to remain in one place in the air while feeding or while looking for a meal.

Imitate - to copy another bird's song or behavior.

Larvae - the first stage of an insect's life, when it looks like a worm.

Lemming - a small mammal that lives in the Arctic and looks a little like a mouse. Lemmings are a favorite food of the Snowy Owl.

Marmots - a group of thick-bodied mammals with short, bushy tails, about the size of a cat. Marmots, including woodchucks and groundhogs, live in burrows.

Mesa - an area of high, flat land with steep slopes.

Migrate - to move from one area to another as the seasons change.

Migration - the process of moving from one place to another as the seasons change.

Mimic - to copy the song or calls of another bird.

Molt - to shed old feathers and replace them with new feathers. Most birds do this a few at a time.

Morph - one color phase of a bird.

Nape - the back of the neck.

Nest box - a birdhouse or other man-made structure provided for birds to nest in.

Nocturnal - active and feeding at night.

Perch - *verb*, to rest on a branch or other object. *Noun*, a branch, wire, pole, or other object on which a bird sits.

Pesticide - a poisonous chemical used to kill weeds or insects.

Phrase - two or more notes that make up a short section of a song.
Pigeon milk - a substance produced in the crops of both male and female doves and pigeons that is fed to their young birds.
Pitch - how high or low a sound is.
Plumage - feathers.
Prey - an animal killed for food by another animal.
Race - a distinct group within a bird species, marked by some difference. The feather color, eye color, bill color, or song may be different.
Range - the full area in which a bird can be found.
Roost - *verb,* the name for a bird's rest or sleep period.
Ruff - a band of feathers around a bird's neck that it can fluff up.
Rump - the area just above the tail on the back of a bird.
Savannah - an open plain with no trees.
Scrub - short, scraggly trees or bushes growing close together.
Secretive - shy; tends to hide.
Shelter - a place that provides protection from the weather and predators.
Silhouette - the outline of a bird, seen against bright light, so all you see is its shape.

Species - a specific kind of plant or animal. A group of birds that are alike and can produce babies are members of the same species.
Suet - beef fat. Often suet is melted into grease and mixed with cornmeal or birdseed to make suet cakes, which make good food for birds.
Talons - long, sharp claws.
Territory - an area a bird claims as its own.
Threatened - a species that is in trouble and may become extinct if steps are not taken to help it. It is against the law to own or hurt a threatened species.
Throat pouch - a bag like flap of skin under the chin of some bird species. It may be used to attract a female, carry food, or cool off.
Trill - a rapid series of notes, a warbling sound.
Tundra - large areas in the Arctic regions that are mostly flat and have no trees.
Warm-blooded - having a body temperature that stays the same, no matter what the surrounding temperature is.
Wattle - bumpy skin, without feathers and often brightly colored, on the heads of some birds, including turkeys and pheasants.

Index

A

Anhinga 28
Avocet, American 44

B

Blackbird, Red-
winged 149
Bluebird, Eastern 114
Bobolink 148
Bobwhite, Northern 63
Bufflehead 36
Bunting, Indigo 141
Painted 142

C

Cardinal, Northern
138
Catbird, Gray 118
Chat, Yellow-
breasted 130
Chickadee, Black-
capped 105
Carolina 104
Coot, American 40
Cormorant, Double-
crested 27
Cowbird, Brown-
headed 153
Crane, Sandhill 23
Creeper, Brown 109
Crossbill, Red 144
Crow, American 100
Cuckoo, Yellow-billed
90

D

Dove, Mourning 65
Rock 64
Duck, Ruddy 38
Wood 32

E

Eagle, Bald 69
Egret, Cattle 18
Great 17

F

Falcon, Peregrine 74
Finch, House 143
Flicker, Northern 88
Flycatcher, Least 92

G

Gallinule, Purple 39
Gnatcatcher, Blue-
gray 113
Goldfinch, American
146
Goose, Canada 30
Snow 29
Grackle, Boat-tailed
152
Common 151
Grebe, Pied-billed 25
Grosbeak, Blue 140
Rose-breasted 139
Guillemot, Black 58
Gull, Great Black-
backed 55
Herring 54
Laughing 52
Ring-billed 53

H

Harrier, Northern 70
Hawk, Red-tailed 72
Sharp-shinned 71
Heron, Black-
crowned Night- 20
Great Blue 16
Green 19

Hummingbird, Ruby-
throated 83

I

Ibis, White 21

J

Jay, Blue 99
Junco, Dark-eyed 137

K

Kestrel, American 73
Killdeer 42
Kingbird, Eastern 94
Kingfisher, Belted 91
Kinglet, Ruby-
crowned 112
Kite, Swallow-tailed
68

L

Lark, Horned 103
Loon, Common 24

M

Mallard 33
Martin, Purple 96
Meadowlark, Eastern
150
Merganser, Common
37
Mockingbird, Northern
119

N

Nighthawk, Common
80
Nuthatch, Red-breasted
107
White-breasted 108

O

Oriole, Baltimore 155
  Orchard 154
Osprey 67
Ovenbird 128
Owl, Barn 75
  Barred 79
  Eastern Screech- 76
  Great Horned 77
  Snowy 78
Oystercatcher, American 43

P

Parula, Northern 123
Pelican, Brown 26
Pheasant, Ring-necked 60
Phoebe, Eastern 93
Plover, Semipalmated 41
Ptarmigan, Willow 61
Puffin, Atlantic 59

R

Redstart, American 127
Robin, American 117

S

Sanderling 49
Sandpiper, Least 50
  Spotted 47
Sapsucker, Yellow-bellied 86
Scaup, Lesser 35
Shoveler, Northern 34
Shrike, Loggerhead 95
Siskin, Pine 145
Snipe, Common 51
Sparrow, Chipping 133
  House 147
  Savannah 134
  Song 135
  White-throated 136
Starling, European 121
Stork, Wood 22
Swallow, Barn 98
  Tree 97
Swan, Mute 31
Swift, Chimney 82

T

Tanager, Scarlet 131
Tern, Common 56
  Forster's 57
Thrasher, Brown 120
Thrush, Swainson's 115
  Wood 116

Titmouse, Tufted 106
Towhee, Eastern 132
Turkey, Wild 62
Turnstone, Ruddy 48

V

Vireo, Blue-headed 101
  Red-eyed 102
Vulture, Turkey 66

W

Warbler, Black-and-white 126
  Yellow 124
  Yellow-rumped 125
Waxwing, Cedar 122
Whip-poor-will 81
Willet 46
Woodpecker, Downy 87
  Pileated 89
  Red-bellied 85
  Red-headed 84
Wren, Carolina 110
  House 111

Y

Yellowlegs, Greater 45
Yellowthroat, Common 129

Picture Credits
Abbreviations: m = male, f = female, t = top, b = bottom, c = center, l = left, r = right.
Plumage illustrations: Simone End, Carl Salter.
Other illustrations: Svetlana Belotserkovskaya 151f; **Ernie Eldredge** 6bl, 6bc, 6br, 7bl, 7br; Melanie Magee 7bc.
Jacket photographs: Front: Ron Austing Wood Duck, Tufted Titmouse, Scarlet Tanager; **Mike Danzenbaker** Atlantic Puffin; **Telegraph Colour Library: J P Fruchet**, grass; **Back: Ron Austing** Barn Owl. **Inside photographs: Fred J. Alsop III** 14b 145; **Ron Austing** 14tl, 14c, 14b, 15b, 16, 17, 18, 19, 21, 22, 23, 28f, 29, 30, 32m & f, 35m, 36m & f, 37m & f, 38m & f, 40, 41, 42, 43, 44, 46, 47, 48, 52, 53, 54, 55, 56, 60m & f, 62m & f, 63f, 64, 67, 68, 70m & f, 71, 72, 73m & f, 75, 76, 77, 78m, 79, 80, 81, 82, 83m & f, 84, 85m & f, 86, 87, 88, 89m & f, 90, 91m & f, 92, 95, 97, 98, 99, 100, 101, 102, 103, 104, 106, 107m & f, 108, 110, 111, 112m & f, 113m, 114f, 115, 116, 117m & f, 118, 119, 120, 121, 122, 123, 124m & f, 125m & f, 126, 128, 129m & f, 130, 131m & f, 132m & f, 133, 134, 137m & f, 138m & f, 139m & f, 140m & f, 141m, 142m & f, 143m & f, 146m & f, 147f, 148f, 149m & f, 150, 152m & f, 153m & f, 154m & f, 155m; **Mike Danzenbaker** 51, 59; **DK Picture Library**/Dennis Avon 63m, 65; Simon Battersby 6t; Mike Dunning 69; Frank Greenaway 74; Cyril Laubscher 20, 66, 147m; Karl & Steve Maslowski 93, 94, 105, 109, 114m, 135, 136, 148m; Kim Taylor 33m & f; Jerry Young 78f; **Frank Lane Picture Agency**/P. Reynolds 58; **Kevin T. Karlson** 31, 34m & f, 45; **Helen H. Kittinger** 15t, 15c; **Brian E. Small** 26, 27, 28m, 35f, 49, 50, 57, 96m & f, 113f, 127m & f, 141f, 144m, 151m, 155f; **Tom Vezo** 11cl, 11cr, 11b, 24, 25, 39, 61m & f.